REINCARNATION AS A CHRISTIAN HOPE

Christian teaching about what the Creed calls 'the life of the world to come' is more muddled than is any other part of traditional doctrine. Professor Mac-Gregor notes at the outset the uneasiness that many of us in the West feel about the notion of reincarnation. It is often misunderstood in a primitivistic and magical way; even in its most ethical and developed forms it seems to fit Christianity about as badly as would a stupa or pagoda atop a Gothic church.

Yet the promise of resurrection, that most central and orthodox of all Christian doctrines, is the promise of a *form* of reincarnation. Most of the difficulties, philosophical and theological, that apply to the one (e.g. memory and continuity) affect the other no less. MacGregor also uses reincarnation as an interpretation of the Anglican doctrine of purgatory as a place of growth.

Dr MacGregor proposes that a careful examination of the roots of reincarnationist theory in the West and its immense and pervasive influence in Christian literature, not least during and since the Italian Renaissance, will show how reincarnation may not only fit into, but also immeasurably enrich, our Christian hope so as to make even educated conservative opinion hospitable to it. He asks both that theologians will consider his proposal with the seriousness he believes it merits and that the average Christian whom he has especially in mind will find it as exciting and rewarding as he does.

Geddes MacGregor, D ès L (Sorbonne), D Phil, DD (Oxford), LL B (Edinburgh), is Emeritus Distinguished Professor of Philosophy, University of Southern California, where he was Dean of the School of Religion. A native of Scotland, he began professional life as Senior Assistant at St Giles', Edinburgh, to the Dean of the Chapel Royal in Scotland. He held a Glasgow parish for several years, served in the British Civil Defence during the Second World War and as Chaplain to the Red Cross, and taught in the Department of Logic, University of Edinburgh.

In 1949 he accepted an invitation to be the first Rufus Jones Professor of Philosophy and Religion at Bryn Mawr, USA, where he remained until his California appointment in 1960. He is a recipient of the California Literature Award (Gold Medal) and of the honorary degree of LHD from Hebrew Union, a member of Mensa and several professional societies, and he has been Special Preacher in many pulpits, including St Paul's, London, and Westminster Abbey. He has been a Visiting Fellow at Yale, Canon Theologian of Los Angeles, and has travelled extensively in Europe and Asia. He is the author of twenty-five books, the first of which was published by Macmillan in 1947.

REINCARNATION AS A CHRISTIAN HOPE

Geddes MacGregor

Barnes & Noble Books
Totowa, New Jersey

First published in the U.S.A. 1982 by
BARNES & NOBLE BOOKS
81, Adams Drive, Totowa,
New Jersey, 07512
ISBN 0-389-20220-7

Printed in Hong Kong

Library of Congress Cataloging in Publication Data

MacGregor, Geddes.
  Reincarnation as a Christian hope.
  (Library of philosophy and religion)
  1. Christianity and reincarnation. I. Title.
II. Series.
BR115.R4M29 1982   236'.2   81-8013
ISBN 0-389-20220-7   AACR2

TO MY WIFE
FOR OUR FORTIETH ANNIVERSARY
IN HAC VITA

Other books by Geddes MacGregor

The Nicene Creed Illumined by Modern Thought
Scotland Forever Home
Gnosis
Reincarnation in Christianity
He Who Lets Us Be
The Rhythm of God
Philosophical Issues in Religious Thought
So Help Me God
A Literary History of the Bible
The Sense of Absence
God Beyond Doubt
The Hemlock and the Cross
The Coming Reformation
Introduction to Religious Philosophy
The Bible in the Making
Corpus Christi
The Thundering Scot
The Vatican Revolution
The Tichborne Impostor
From a Christian Ghetto
Les Frontières de la morale et de la religion
Christian Doubt
Aesthetic Experience in Religion

Contents

Preface

The state of teaching about 'the life of the world to come' has been for long the most confused aspect of Christian theology. The concept of reincarnation tends to alarm even the most heterodox of Christians. Yet the promise of resurrection, that most central of Christian doctrines, is a promise of a *form* of reincarnation. The most important difficulties, philosophical and theological, that apply to the one affect the other no less. Although some Christians account my attitude to and interpretation of the fundamental doctrines of the Christian faith too orthodox for their liking, I am inclined to take very seriously the possibility that a form of reincarnationism might show how sadly we have neglected what could be an enrichment of the Christian hope. Christians of more heterodox opinions may find themselves even more easily attracted to the proposal. I address myself, therefore, to educated Christians of every shade of opinion.

When I was invited some years ago to give the Birks Lectures at McGill University, Montreal, the Dean and Faculty chose, among some suggestions of mine, a series entitled 'The Christening of Karma' which later developed into a book published under the title *Reincarnation in Christianity*. More recently I was invited to give the Florence B. Warren Lectures at the University of Dubuque on a similar subject. When, therefore, my old friend Professor John Hick asked me to provide the present book, based on these lectures, for the series he edits with my first publisher, I accepted with much pleasure.

In biblical references I have generally followed the Jerusalem Bible (JB), but in some instances the New English Bible (NEB) or the King James Version (KJV).

Los Angeles   Geddes MacGregor
July 1981

Acknowledgements

The author and publishers wish to thank the following who have kindly given permission for the use of copyright material: Hutchinson Publishing Group for the verse from 'Pre-Existence' in *Collected Poems* by Frances Cornford; and the Society of Authors as the literary representative of the Estate of John Masefield and Macmillan Publishing Company Inc. for the verse from *A Creed*.

1 The Nature and Importance of the Question

I still have many things to say to you
but they would be too much for you now.

I have been telling you all this in metaphors,
the hour is coming
when I shall no longer speak to you in metaphor;
but tell you about the Father in plain words.

John 16.12 and 25 (JB)

Reincarnation is by any reckoning an odd and alien, not to say exotic, concept to most Christian minds. The notion is strange, foreign-sounding, even a little weird to many of us in the West. Even to those Christians who are accustomed to think of themselves as open-minded and liberal in their understanding of their faith it usually seems as ill-fitting as a pagoda atop a Gothic church, while conservative Christians view it with horror if not alarm.

The reason is simple. At least the immediate cause of the general discomfort provoked by the notion is easily identified. Reincarnation is associated with India and those oriental religions, such as Buddhism, that were originally cradled in that sub-continent and have spread to other parts of Asia. It is certainly true that reincarnationism is so much a part of the furnishings of the Indian mind that no one brought up within the orbit of that influence can entirely escape it. You can almost sniff it in the air as in Italy you smell the fragrance of flowers and the odour of garlic. Moreover, it tends to be geared to pantheistic and other metaphysical presuppositions that are plainly alien to the mainstream of Christian tradition, for Christianity, like Judaism and Islam, has a heritage of uncompromising monotheism. Scholarly Christians, who are even more acutely aware of such differences, are therefore, in general, as disinclined as are any others to take the possibility seriously that a form of reincarnationism might be compatible with the Christian heritage.

1

I have said 'a form of' reincarnationism, for as we shall see in a later chapter there are several ways of understanding the term. For the moment let us be content to note a basic difference. Reincarnation, no less than other ideas in the history of the religions of the world, has been understood in primitive and in highly developed ways. In folklore the idea appears as part of a magical understanding of things. By the whim of a wicked witch the handsome prince is turned into a frog and by the equally capricious and arbitrary command of a fairy godmother the frog is turned back again into the prince. Not only is reincarnation associated at that level with such metamorphoses; the danger exists that evil agencies, either out of spite for your having somehow offended them or for no particular reason at all, may have you reincarnated as a dog or a pig. It may take you a long time, moreover, to learn how to get out of such a mess, for in the power-play of cosmic politics skills are not learned in a day. There are no rational rules; it is, rather, a question of studying the psychology of gods and demons so as to turn such knowledge to your personal advantage and eventual advancement in relation to the Pantheon. Reincarnationism at this level is a widespread phenomenon and it is natural that one should account its intrusion into Christian thought as a ridiculous and perhaps even blasphemous enterprise. Part of the *raison d'être* of Christianity is, indeed, to liberate us from such enslavements of the mind.

Very different, however, is the highly ethical understanding of reincarnation that prevails in Indian thought. In this heritage the individual in his loneliness is absolutely responsible for the manner in which his life develops over the course of millions of incarnations. The karmic principle is inexorable. It is the moral law and is presented very much, *mutatis mutandis*, as Kant presented the moral law in his *Critique of Practical Reason*. That law is predetermined; it is at the heart of all things and is as unalterable as is the nature of 'the starry heavens'. The individual, however, is free to act as he will. Contrary to what superficial observers in the West have often supposed, there is no fatalism in the individual's confrontation with the karmic law. He or she can make or mar his or her life and destiny. The individual in the course of previous lives has by his or her own actions inherited good karma or bad, expressed in the circumstances he or she must face in this life; birth into an intelligent and noble family, for instance, or into that of slaves, a healthy body or a diseased one, and so forth. Adverse circumstances need not be interpreted as punishment, however; they are simply the circumstances needed for further development. God gives each one of us a task to do, as we might put the case in our Christian way. By the same token, what the world calls favourable circumstances may be an obstacle rather than a blessing. We shall have an opportunity of examining more exactly how the karmic principle works. For the present let us simply note that the working of it is nothing if not ethical.

We shall also at a much later stage consider the obvious objection likely to spring to Christian minds: is not such an far too much a salvation-by-works outlook to be at all compatible with the strong emphasis on grace that is typical of all Christian theology, whether presented in a 'Catholic' or a 'Protestant' form? For the moment we ought to note merely that the notion of a moral law, whether as presented by Kant or in the Upanishads, is by no means alien to Christianity: the Torah or Mosaic Law, which the psalmist lauds as 'perfect, converting the soul', is the very foundation of the Christian Way. Jesus insisted that his purpose was not to destroy the Law, the Torah, but to fulfil or complete it. So that objection cannot be in itself an objection to reincarntion as a possible ingredient in Christian theology.

All the great religions of the world purport in one way or another to save their votaries, if not all humankind, from destruction. All promise in one way or another salvation. That is indeed the *raison d'être* of every great religion. Although a religion may work from this or that set of presuppositions and may envisage this or that as 'ultimate reality' or God and may erect this or that kind of doctrinal structure, the heart of every religion is its programme of salvation. As medical practitioners may follow this or that kind of methodology (the Chinese traditionally use acupuncture, for instance, and in the West osteopaths use methods that are not approved in conventional medical schools), so religious teachers have their own methods of attaining the goals they set. What is in no doubt in either case is the goal: in medicine it is the healing of the patient; in religion it is the saving of what is traditionally called 'the soul'. From what precisely we are being saved is always debatable, as is the destiny of men and women. The essential purpose of religion remains. There is no doubt about it. It is fundamental: the salvation of souls.

In Christianity all this is strikingly the case. Christians have argued and still argue vigorously about details of the theological scenery, about the aetiology of the disease that made redemption necessary, and about the methods of reaching the goal; but all are agreed, be they Baptists or Greek Orthodox, Lutherans or Presbyterians, Roman Catholics or Anglicans, Congregationalists or Quakers, Salvationists or Pentecostalists, that we sorely and urgently need to be saved from a terrible fate (whether it be called extinction or hell or anything else) and that the basic aim is to attain that salvation.

No Christian dare be in any doubt, therefore, of what his or her religion is about. It is first and last about 'being saved'. When it comes to asking, however, what precisely salvation means, educated Christians must pause for reflection. Up to a point the priest may follow the medical practitioner who can tell his patient: 'When the pain has gone you feel better, don't you? That is what I am trying to do for you.' So the priest can say, in effect: 'You perceive that you are loaded down by your sense of guilt, which is due to your alienation from God, the Source of all Good. We are going to get you back on the track again and put you right with God. Therein lies your salvation.' Neither the priest nor the physician, however, can be satisfied with so glib an answer. Many a cancer patient and many a person on the verge of a heart attack feels all right, perhaps indeed better than ever he or she has ever felt before. So the patient's question must always be: 'But what exactly are you saving me from — premature death? terrible pain? general deterioration of my health? And what exactly is your aim for me? Where precisely are you taking me? I don't want to be treated as a child. I want to know where I am supposed to be going.'

Similarly, the intelligent Christian cannot be content with generalizations such as: 'Your soul is in mortal danger, but by the grace of God and the use of the holy sacraments of the Church you are going to be saved through the Cross of Christ. You will eventually reach eternal bliss in heaven.' A parade of questions passes through the hearer's mind; too many, indeed, to be put to anyone at any one time. The old imagery of heavenly bliss, the harps and the crystal rivers, the pearly gates and the streets of gold, may not be entirely useless, but it is certainly far from meeting the case. Besides, how precisely is it supposed to fit with what we know about the nature of the universe, and especially the evolutionary development in nature? We have long ago abandoned (if we ever accepted) notions such as Archbishop Ussher's that humanity was created on a specific day such as according to his calculations a day in October, 4004 BC. All that we have learned of the evolutionary character of the life-process excludes the possibility that a determinable date can be assigned to the creation of man as one can be assigned to, say, the Battle of Agincourt or the passing of the Bill of Rights. We have had to re-think our understanding of the past. Must we not also, however, re-think our understanding of the future?

By that I do not mean, of course, that we are to pretend to foresee the future or to predict how things will turn out in any individual case. Yet if we have been able to claim to interpret our evolutionary past in Christian terms, as has been done by Teilhard de Chardin, for example, and many of Teilhard's British and American predecessors in the late nineteenth and early twentieth centuries, surely we ought to do better than pearly gates, purgatorial fires, and infernal furnaces for our Christian vision of the future. As we shall see in our next chapter, traditional Christian doctrine about 'the life of the world to come', whether couched in popular images such as these or in more scholarly terms, is extraordinarily confused. It is probably the most confused of all branches of Christian theology. Unfortunately, it is and never can be merely a side issue for Christians. It is central to Christian faith. Without it there is no distinctive Christian hope that would give that faith any point at all. In the course of the study on which we are embarking we may hope to see some reasons why reincarnation in some form might be a plausible, even felicitous, perhaps even necessary way of understanding what lies in store for us. We shall also of course, see some reasons to the contrary. At any rate, we may certainly hope to see the whole question in better perspective so that we can make up our own minds about it. We shall understand better, moreover, why the Church came to frown, or at any rate to seem to frown, on such notions. I say 'to seem to frown' because there is no entirely clear evidence that reincarnationism was ever definitely, unequivocally condemned by any official organ of the Church, although there have been pronouncements that have seemed to reject it by implication.

We shall also have to reckon with the extraordinary vitality the concept has exhibited in the West and its remarkable persistence in an intellectual climate that has been generally, as we have already noted, assumed to be inhospitable to it. We shall see much later in our study that reincarnationist notions in the West were by

no means confined to groups that the Church accounted heretical,
such as the Bogomils and the Albigenses, but have appeared in
various guises (in the Middle Ages mostly underground but later
very openly) as the opinions of men of the greatest distinction in
European and American literature: in Germany, Goethe; in the
United States, Emerson; in England, Masefield; in Ireland, Yeats.
That is to mention but a few random instances. Among
Renaissance thinkers and poets it was a prevalent idea stimulated
in part, no doubt, by the recovery of the ancient sources of the
humanist tradition, which was a tradition by no means lacking in
religious awareness. This tradition included, of course, Plato,
whose acceptance of a Pythagorean tradition of reincarnationism
as part of his own heritage of thought is well known. Wherever that
Platonic tradition exerted its influence, which was almost
everywhere among both the friends and the foes of the Church,
reincarnationism could not easily have been outside the general
mental picture.

The fact that Plato's influence was very pervasive in the history
of European thought directs our attention at once to the
circumstances in which Christianity was cradled, for there, too,
Platonic and other influences had already been at work even in the
half-hellenised Judaism into which Jesus was born. When it was
carried by Paul and others to the Gentile world and interpreted, as
inevitably it had to be, in terms of the fashionable philosophies of
the day, the influence of Platonic and, later, of Neoplatonic ideas
was such as cannot be ignored. True, it can be exaggerated; but
even when one is exercising the greatest caution and scholarly
restraint one must face the fact that reincarnationism, through
Platonic influences or otherwise, was so much in the air about the
time of Christ that it would be unthinkable that it should not have
played a part in the beliefs and hopes of seekers of salvation. What
is surprising is, rather, that we do not hear even more of it in early
Christian literature than we do. We do, however, find more of it
than many people suppose, and to this point we shall also address
ourselves later.

The Christian who is biblically oriented, as surely all Christians
ought to be, naturally asks: if Christ had taught or even permitted
a doctrine such as reincarnation, would not he have clearly said so?
Or, to put the question more subtly: if reincarnation had been an
accepted view or even a permitted option, would not Paul have
said something about it in his letters to the churches scattered

throughout the Mediterranean world, and would not the Evangelists have recorded at least some mention of it by their Lord? In the absence of any specific mention of it as a desirable form of Christian hope or concept of at least a stage in human destiny, are we not entitled to conclude that if it played any part at all in the thought of Jesus and his disciples, it could not have been, or at any rate could not have seemed to the New Testament writers to have been, of any crucial importance?

To this we must reply that the doctrine of the Trinity, which is generally accepted as a central expression of Christian belief about the nature of God, is in a very similar case. Nowhere in the Bible is there any mention of it except in the verse in the first letter of John,[1] which is known to all biblical scholars to be a very late interpolation and is usually omitted from modern translations of the New Testament. Only much later, in the fourth and fifth centuries, was that formulation of the Christian doctrine of God developed and eventually established as official Christian teaching. It was an interpretation, in terms of the intellectual climate of the day, of what the New Testament witnesses to the divine nature. So the objection that reincarnation is not expressly taught in the New Testament carries little or no weight.

In fact, there is nothing we can call New Testament witness to the Christian doctrine of 'the life of the world to come', for no such doctrinal unity is to be found there. On the contrary, what we find in the New Testament is a remarkably wide variety of expectations and visions of human destiny. That all is to be 'put right' morally in the end is clearly taught. That is plainly what the concept of Christ's final judgment implies. There is to be a moral reckoning. In the end the righteousness of God shall prevail over evil. People in the first century who accepted the Christian message generally interpreted the talk of a 'Day' of Judgment as literally a day, as so many have understood the 'day' of man's creation. They expected it to occur at any time. Tomorrow, for example, might well be the day on which the sky would be darkened and the Lord would appear, descending from the heavens to sit in judgment over all humankind. On that day the sheep and the goats, that is, the righteous and the wicked, would be judged and separated and consigned to their respective destinations: a terrible day for the goats, a day of unspeakable joy for the sheep.

Wherever such a literalistic understanding prevailed, reincarnation would not fit. Such a literalistic understanding was in fact

very common in the first century. So the poetic ways of expressing
the fate of humankind (crystal rivers for the righteous and fiery
furnaces with gnashing of teeth for the wicked) raised no fundamental questions in the minds of those who accepted that literalistic way of understanding the Day of Judgment. Nor did the very
varied understandings of immortality and resurrection that played
their part in the thought of the New Testament writers present to
such people the puzzles they tend to present to us, for what
mattered was the Day of Judgment and the victory of God over the
Devil, not the details of the future of humankind. As they had no
notion of the evolutionary process that had brought man to his
then present condition, so they could not seek, as surely a modern
Christian must, to understand something of how, in the continuing process, salvation is to be worked out.

What we have already been able to consider in a perfunctory
way in this introductory chapter should bring home to us at least
one important point: the kind of question about 'the life of the
world to come' that comes naturally to Christians today would not
have come so readily into the minds of first-century Christians
unless these minds had already been in some way prepared for it.
Lacking our understanding of the evolutionary process they could
not have raised it at all *in the way* we must surely raise it today. The
question before us, 'Is any form of reincarnationism compatible
with the fundamental beliefs of orthodox Christians?' is plainly a
modern question that we could not expect anyone to have asked at
that time, for there was no clearly defined body of Christian
theology to be related to it. Yet they could not have raised any
question about reincarnationism unless it had been already in
their mental background.

That it was at least to some extent in that background must be
among the points we have to consider. I think there is some
substantial evidence that it was; but if so it would have presented
itself to first-century Christians very differently from the way in
which it strikes us, especially because of our awareness of the
evolutionary nature of the creation of life, but also by reason of our
being able and compelled to survey the now long history of
Christian thought.

Nevertheless, we ought to note at the outset that the resurrection
hope, which was by all accounts central in the thinking of these
ancient Christians, is itself a *kind* of reincarnationism. Paul urges
us to expect to receive a 'glorified' body. The resurrection of Christ

has made that a Christian's proper expectation. That is certainly not reincarnationism as found either in primitive folklore or in the much more sophisticated disquisitions of the Upanishads; but it does present us with the notion of relinquishing at death the body we now have and assuming another one later on. True, the resurrection body is envisaged as 'glorified'. The presumption is that it is not expected to be of flesh (*sarx*). Nevertheless it is understood to be an organization that will relate to me as does the present organization of my body (*sōma*) relate to me now. Such a conception is entirely compatible with any reincarnationist doctrine that is imaginative enough to go beyond the limitations of our present human structure to something beyond it. Now that we have learned something of the vastness of the galaxies, we can see the probability that somewhere other than on this middle-sized planet of the cosmic backwater which we parochially call the solar system are to be found other beings, some more fully developed than we. The bodies of such beings might very well be much less gross than ours. Ours are, indeed, an odd mixture: from one stand-point so many pounds of fat and pints of water; from another, extraordinarily intricate, with thirty-five miles of glomerular capillaries in a pair of kidneys and twelve billion neurons in a cauliflower-shaped brain whose 'telephone connections' are estimated to be of the order of 1 000 000 000 000 000 000 000 000. A body that comprises such complex arrangements is indeed 'glorified' compared with that of a worm or even a mouse, so the notion of an even finer disposition need not much strain our imagination.

'But, you may ask,' writes Paul, 'how are the dead raised? In what kind of body? How foolish! The seed you sow does not come to life unless it has first died; and what you sow is not the body that shall be, but a naked grain . . . All flesh is not the same flesh: there is flesh of men, flesh of beasts, of birds, and of fishes — all different. There are heavenly bodies and earthly bodies; and the splendour of the heavenly bodies is one thing, the splendour of the earthly, another. The sun has a splendour of its own, the moon another splendour, and the stars another, for star differs from star in brightness. So it is with the resurrection of the dead.'[2] While the apostle is not, of course, thinking of a schema such as we would associate with reincarnationism, what he writes to the Corinthians would be peculiarly apposite to a highly developed form of reincarnationist teaching such as we might have in mind.

The modern philosophical and scientific objections to the notion of an 'inner self' that 'survives' one body at death and later assumes another are formidable. Some attention will be given to them in two later chapters. Indian thought long ago provided ingenious solutions of its own. Solutions in terms of what we now know from quantum physics about energy and mass seem by no means out of the question, although the mind-body problem is still one of the most intransigent. At the outset, however, we must note that any difficulties of this kind that attend the notion of reincarnation apply just as much to a doctrine of resurrection such as is at the heart of New Testament teaching about the future life. So no objection of this kind need deter us from a reincarnationist view if it has not already deterred us from a traditionalist doctrine of resurrection.

Traditionally, however, resurrection has been generally understood as pertaining to a final state. There is no doubt that most first-century Christians, expecting the end of the world to be imminent, would have tended to presuppose that the new age would be attained by an abrupt change on the Day of Judgment, leading to a state of affairs that would be properly called 'permanent' in comparison with the supposedly brief history of humankind since the day of its creation. In a non-evolutionary understanding of the life process this, as we have already seen, would have been natural. When that hope of the imminence of the *parousia* had faded, the notion of an intermediate state attracted the attention of thinkers such as Clement of Alexandria and eventually played an extremely important part in the Church's thought and life. Purgatory, despite the unfortunate ecclesiastical abuses associated with it, especially in the late Middle Ages, became, in the confusing chaos of teachings about human destiny and the future life, by far the most intelligible.

Most of us today, however we may couch the expression of our thoughts and feelings, tend to be just as convinced as were our Christian forebears centuries ago that for one reason or another we need more time to work out our salvation. The notion of one's being plunged into a few years of trial (a span of life varying from a hundred years or more in a few cases to a mere day or two in others, with average life expectancy nowadays notably increasing), as a result of which we are to be judged worthy of everlasting bliss in heaven or no less interminable torture in hell, seems to most thoughtful people not only fantastic but unmerciful if not unjust.

Students complain, not without cause, that under a rigorous examination system the entire course of their lives is to a considerable degree determined by their performance in one examination extending over a mere week or so. The theological notion that one life of indeterminate duration but at the best notoriously brief should be the basis for so awesomely momentous a judgment is not one that could ever have appealed to thoughtful Christians as expressive of the love of God for his creatures. So the notion of a second chance (or, better, of a series of chances) is one that accords with what is to be expected by those who accept the biblical revelation that God's ways, however mysterious, are in the long run seen to be compassionate and morally constructive. Such a schema might well be the best way for a Christian today to construe the ancient doctrine of purgatory, that pilgrimage of purification and growth that fits us for whatever lies beyond it.

I hope that in this introductory chapter enough has been said to convince the reader that at least the concept of reincarnation need not be rejected out of hand by Christians who wish to remain fundamentally loyal to Christ and his Church. Plainly, however, such a proposal demands both historical investigation and theological examination before the reader can judge the merits and demerits of the case.

2 Confusion in Traditional Christian Options About 'The Life of the World to Come'

Good Master, what must I do win eternal (*aiōnios*) life?
Mark 10.17 (NEB)

Behind every literature in the world, whether it be accounted 'sacred' or 'profane' lies a cultural ancestry and a history of ideas. The New Testament, which is that part of early Christian literature that came to be recognized by the Church *c.* AD 200 as canonical, that is, regular and ecclesiastically approved, is no exception. Not only were all the New Testament writers steeped in the outlook of their Jewish heritage; Jesus, the focus of their testimony as of their lives, was thoroughly grounded in the Law, the Prophets, and the Writings that together make up what Christians call the Old Testament. He habitually alluded to it and often quoted from it. This literary heritage was not only remarkably complex in the sense that it had passed through centuries of editorial development; it was also expressive of a variety of points of view. Its components ranged from classical elements that had emerged in an ancient period, when life was simple and ideas were both primitive and parochial, to comparatively recent elements such as the book of Daniel and those writings that modern scholars recognize as part of what they call the Wisdom literature. This later part of the Old Testament reflects foreign influences and a broader outlook than could have been possible for an isolated society such as that of the ancient Hebrews.

Between the Old Testament and the New there is, moreover, a gap of more than a century and a half. The thought, outlook, and speculations of that intervening period are expressed in what

12

modern Christian scholars call intertestamental literature. This background has come to be seen as peculiarly important for an understanding of the rise of Christianity. However 'conservative' or 'liberal' we account our view, it is a background with which we have to reckon. Above all, we must recognize that there was nothing monolithic about the thought or outlook of Jews in the time of Christ. The Law or Torah was indeed specially venerated, as it still is by Jews today; but by the time of Christ Jewish thought had been immensely modified and enriched by the influx of foreign ideas both from Babylonia and from the Mediterranean world. Even in so closed a society as Palestine sought to be, its frequent subjection to foreign armies of occupation was one of the factors that ensured an influx of ideas and ways that would have seemed strange and outlandish to people in the days of the patriarchs of old.

To say that the Christian Way emerged in a very Jewish am-bierce of life and thought is certainly true; but it was by that time a 'ewishness that had been profoundly affected by the thought of the Greek-speaking Mediterranean world. For example, it was the practice of the armies of occupation to billet their soldiers in private homes, so that even in Palestine ordinary folk about the time of Christ would inevitably have learned some Greek, which was by then an international language, somewhat as English is today. With the words would come some of the ideas that were being then currently canvassed.

More importantly still, Jews had been by this time already widely dispersed through that larger world. It was for such Jews that the Bible had been translated about the year 250 BC into the Greek of the version called the Septuagint, which was the version generally followed by the New Testament writers when they quoted the ancient Scriptures. The outlook of many Jews in the time of Christ was as different from that of their forefathers in the Jewish homeland as is the outlook of, say, a fourth- or fifth-generation American of Roumanian extraction different from that of his Roumanian ancestors. When he returned to the Homeland the cultural shock would have been notable. Some understanding of all this is crucial for an understanding of the complexity of opinions about the afterlife that were current in the time of Christ.

The Hebrews in earlier times, like the Greeks of, say, Homer's day, had harboured the vague, primitivistic notions typical of most societies at a certain stage of their development. The dead, according to that early view, went to Sheol, a shadowy place, probably conceived much as was the Greek Hades, its counterpart. It was an underground place: Heaven was above, Sheol below, and the earth in between. Nor were they very consistent in their talk about Sheol. No doubt they were just as hazy about 'down there in Sheol' as many Christians have been about 'up there in Heaven'. Sometimes they use the term as synonymous with the grave. Sometimes it is indeed no more than a euphemism for death itself, again much as an old-fashioned person today might say of a friend that he or she has 'gone to Heaven'. When they did picture Sheol it was not a very pleasing prospect: a sort of non-world of darkness and dust. Presumably the Hebrews and many other peoples would have applauded Homer when he said that he would rather be a beggar in the present life than a king in the land of shades. For in Sheol there is neither knowledge nor activity nor thought,[1] nor even praise of the Lord.[2] To say, as does the psalmist, that 'If I climb the heavens, you are there, there too, if I lie in Sheol',[3] is somewhat like our saying that God is everywhere, in the uttermost galaxies as in the vast emptinesses of space.

Very different is the spectrum of ideas in the Judaism into which Jesus was born. In his milieu it was not surprising to find a rich man asking, as did the one reported by Mark: 'Good Master, what must I do to win eternal life?' For many thoughtful people, Jewish and Gentile, were asking that sort of question. They were eager to avoid the abhorrent fate of extinction and to obtain instead the power to attain endless (*aiōnios*) life. The mere fact that anyone was by then able to ask the kind of question the rich man in the Gospel asked shows how the attitude to such matters had changed. A new world of ideas had opened up. To have asked questions of this kind, about immortality or resurrection or any other such concept, in the time of, say, Moses or even Amos, would have been as unlikely as Shakespeare's asking questions about the possibility of space travel.

By the time of Jesus a wide variety of speculations about the afterlife had been bandied about. There were many options. For instance, as we read in Acts, the Pharisees believed in the resurrection of the dead; the Sadducees did not.[4] The concept of immortality in the sense of an intrinsically immortal soul independent of the body, conceived as its temporary house or dress, was alien to classic Hebrew tradition but was widespread in the Mediterranean world as it has been and still is in India. It had received the blessing of Plato. Reincarnationist ideas were also widespread in the general clearing house of available religious notions. All these ideas, as we shall presently see, affected early Christian thought.

Nevertheless, the New Testament writers did think in a Jewish mould. Paul, for example, follows a Jewish tradition in conceptualising a plurality of heavens. The Hebrew word is plural: *shamāyim*. So he could talk as he did of having been carried up into the third heaven, in the course of an ecstatic experience he claimed to have enjoyed.[5] Sometimes the third heaven was identified with Paradise. The word 'paradise' (Greek *paradeisos*, Hebrew *pardēs*) is a loan-word from Old Persian, where it was used to designate a walled garden such as might be found in a royal estate or the like. The Garden of Eden was conceived as such a place: the Hebrew word for garden (*gan*) was rendered in the Septuagint *paradeisos*. In the later thought of the Hebrews the hope of a return to such a blissful state was not unnatural. We find, indeed, a tendency in later Judaism to see Sheol as the destiny of the wicked and the nondescript and Paradise as promised to the righteous. There is nothing definite, however, about such an arrangement, and there are many alternative speculations and interpretations. Sheol also comes to be distinguished from Gehenna, which by the time of Christ had become the symbol for the abode of the wicked. The name 'Gehenna' (Hebrew *ge-hinnōm*) referred to a geographical entity that divided ancient Jerusalem from the hills to the south and the west (the modern Wadi el Rababi that joins the Wadi el Nar, the Kidron, at the south of the hill of Zion), which had acquired unpleasant associations as the site where in primitive times human sacrifice had been offered. It became a symbol for the rubbish dump or incinerator where the wicked would be burned like straw.[6]

Paradise, however, could be conceived in various ways. Sometimes the term is used in the Bible in its old, literal sense of 'garden'.[7] It might also represent an intermediate state. That Jesus, when he promised the 'good thief' on the Cross that they would be together in Paradise that very day,[8] was alluding to such an intermediate state seems plausible, since according to the New Testament witnesses more time than that elapsed before his resurrection and much more time before he 'ascended into heaven'. The notion of an intermediate state was apparently not alien to Jewish thought in the century or two before Christ, for we read of prayers for the dead, which implies an intermediate state of some kind, since there is no point in praying for those whose final destiny is already fixed one way or the other. After the Reformation in the sixteenth century this was the consideration that prompted its more vehement partisans to forbid prayers for the dead, since such a practice implied the doctrine of purgatory which, because of its corruption in the late Middle Ages, they vigorously opposed. It was the notion of such an intermediate state that had been developed from as early as the second century of the Christian era into the doctrine of purgatory.

One thing is clear in early Christian teaching: the lot of the righteous, whatever it may be, is supremely desirable and that of the wicked correspondingly horrible. The precise nature of their respective fates is nevertheless vague and open to several inter-pretations. The book of Daniel refers to resurrection as though it were and had been for long an accepted belief.[9] References to resurrection are quite common in the literature of the period just before the time of Christ,[10] though neither the Samaritans nor the Sadducees, for instance, accepted such a view.[11] In such a fluid situation one could be permitted a wide range of choice about what one believed about the future life. After the death of Christ, however, Christian testimony to and belief in his resurrection was certainly the heart of the Christian *kerygma*, the apostolic proclamation of the Good News. The hope of resurrection became central to Christian belief. Eventually, however, other doctrines less rooted in the specifically Jewish background of the followers of the Christian Way were mixed with it.

We look in vain in the New Testament for any clear enunciation of what precisely we are to understand by resurrection. Indeed, Paul discourages speculations of that sort, on the ground that they are corrosive of true faith.[12] The point seems to be that, with the great Day of Reckoning imminent, a genuine Christian ought rather to be praising God who has made our resurrection possible through the glorious resurrection of Jesus Christ, apart from which no such hope could have been well grounded. The insistence is always simply that we are promised resurrection to *new life*, a better quality or greater dimension of life than we now live. There is no further specification that would enable us to say what the life promised is or is not. If a child is told that the family is going to a much grander house than their present one and to lead a more interesting and richer life there, would not it be churlish to fuss about details such as whether it is to be brick or stone and with sash or casement windows? Probably not, if the promise were for the distant future; but when the move is supposed to be 'any day now' the point would be well taken: rely on your parents who have made the move possible. A loving Christian who trusts God and recognizes Jesus as his Saviour will not be excited to idle curiosity but will, rather, praise God continually for his salvation.

The earliest followers of the Christian Way were of Jewish background and so were in general unaccustomed to the notion that the human soul is intrinsically immortal, indestructible, incapable of annihilation. That was not the mould of thought that came naturally to anybody in the Jewish heritage. Paul seems to assume, indeed, that the ordinary expectation is extinction. 'The wages of sin is death.'[13] Still, he does deplore the opinion of some who argue that the resurrection has already taken place, as Hymenaeus and Philetus were saying.[14] The Christian hope, to those with this background, was not the result of learning about the indestructibility of the soul; on the contrary, it was the result of a surprise, a gift astonishingly bestowed by God on those who had faith in the Lord Jesus.

When the Christian message was carried to the Gentile world, the ears on which it fell had been accustomed to a very different tune. Generally speaking, these Gentile converts had already picked up from one or other of the multitude of schools of thought the notion that the human soul is intrinsically immortal, being a spark of the divine fire that governs the universe. That divine spark is embedded for a time in a flesh-and-blood, animal body, which is not its true home but, rather, a temporary habitation. The purpose of its entry into this body was understood to be in one way or another educative. The body, like any musical or other instrument, is at once a limitation and a servant. It is a prison, yet not a place of retributive punishment but, rather, of correction and education. It is the vehicle with which one is provided to convey one through a pilgrimage to one's destination. Views of this kind were expressed under many guises and there were various versions of them. The Stoic philosophy, influential throughout the Mediterranean world, was one medium for the dissemination of ideas of this sort. Platonic teachings were powerful instruments in creating this general mould of thought among those who were interested in the destiny of the soul.

Throughout that world at that time Gnostic ideas were extraordinarily influential in promoting such a climate of thought. Gnosticism was not a philosophy or a religion in the sense that you could have found a Gnostic church or a Gnostic school; it was an intellectual mood, a spiritual attitude, rather than a specific philosophy or religion. It was, however, a mood and an attitude that engendered a widespread tendency to view life as a pilgrimage and to account the body as an instrument of the soul. Of course most people probably thought little about that and many no doubt disbelieved it; but in the sense in which we say jocosely that a French atheist is a Catholic atheist and a Swedish atheist a Lutheran atheist, so we might perhaps say that unbelievers in the Mediterranean world in the first century were Gnostic unbelievers. Such was the climate that nobody could be entirely unaffected, as nobody in our society today can be entirely unaffected by, say, Freudian ideas, even those who are critical of them.

The notion that the human soul is in a state of pilgrimage and that the body it inhabits is not its true home implies that its true home is beyond this life. If, however, we are pilgrims on the way somewhere, we are also pilgrims who have come from somewhere. The question is not only whither are we bound but whence have we come. The notion of the pre-existence of the soul was already familiar to almost every thinking Gentile who heard the Gospel message and it was destined to play an important part in the thought of some of the great Fathers of the Christian Church. Origen, for example (born *c.* 185), who was probably the greatest biblical scholar of his day and also the greatest speculative thinker in the early Church, was a prominent exponent of the pre-existence of the soul. Clement of Alexandria, his teacher, seems ambivalent on this question, but what he and others say shows at least how lively a question it was among Gentile Christians of the second and third centuries.

The notion that the soul has pre-existed implies not only that its existence is somehow independent of the body but that, since it has inhabited one body at least, it is likely to be on its way to inhabit others. In fact reincarnationist views were among the various options discussed by early Christian thinkers in the Gentile world. Those who championed pre-existence were sometimes called the *pre-existiani*. The vehemence of those who, like Tertullian, for instance, attack their opinions shows how important these opinions were in early Church discussions. We shall consider this and other such matters later. The point to note for the moment is that such was the openness to ideas in the first century or two of the Christian Way that when eventually the hope of the imminent Second Coming of Christ waned and the Church, for various reasons, felt compelled to harden and sharpen her doctrinal position, making it more dogmatically exclusive, the doctrinal confusion concerning the future life was such as could not be disentangled. Oscar Cullmann puts an aspect of the matter succinctly: 'On his missionary journeys Paul surely met people who were unable to believe in his preaching of the resurrection *for the very reason* that they believed in the immortality of the soul. Thus in Athens there was no laughter until Paul spoke of the resurrection.'[15] The Church could not preach to the Gentile world and ignore such practical difficulties.

The result was that various strands of Mediterranean belief about the afterlife were interwoven into the already confused teaching about human destiny. Soon the Church was teaching that, since man has an immortal soul, people should recognize that on their conduct on earth depends the awful choice: heaven or hell. This life provides our only chance. A few years now determines our fate for ever. The urgency of the situation is what every preacher must emphasize. We have an immortal soul, each one of us; it must go somewhere. It is up to us to determine, by our life here on earth, whether it will go to heaven to enjoy everlasting bliss or to hell to be everlastingly tortured in hell fire. Certain kinds of sin (mortal sin) are so grave that they 'kill' the soul, so that it cannot hope to attain heaven; yet because it is indestructible it cannot die and so must be consigned to the only other possible destination. There can be no question of an intermediate state for such a 'lost' soul, because the intermediate state, purgatory, is but a stepping-stone to heaven, for which such a soul has made itself incapable.

Further confusion developed over what happens to a soul immediately at death. The first-century Christians generally supposed that, since the Second Coming was imminent, any Christian who died before it occurred must be accounted simply 'asleep in Christ'. That is the expectation expressed in the typical inscription in the catacombs: *dormit in Christo* or *dormit in pace*. The person, temporarily deprived of a body, was deemed to be in some way preserved in a kind of sleep, protected by Christ till his

return. As time went on and the expectation of the imminent
return of Christ faded, such sentiments continued. Indeed, one
may still see such epitaphs today in modern cemeteries. Others,
however, held that the deceased person had gone to heaven,
receiving there either a temporary resurrection body or else some
means of dispensing with a body until the General Resurrection.

As the doctrine of purgatory developed, the view became
general that the deceased person needed the Church's prayers,
since (although salvation was assured) the time of the purgatorial
sojourn could be diminished by such prayers. Purgatorial time,
however, was held to be different from earthly time and its
working unknown to us, so precisely what such prayers could do
was unknown, except in so far as their effect could be
calculated in terms of what a penance or good work on earth might
accomplish. Also in question was the corporeality or otherwise of
the person during the purgatorial stay. The fires of purgatory were
painful indeed, but whether they were corporeal or otherwise was
never entirely clear. Even more confusing was the state of those
who were destined for eternal punishment in hell. Like all others,
they could not die; but what happened to them before the final
judgement? On that day they would receive back their bodies to
be tormented for ever in hell; but between death and that general
resurrection did they get a temporary body to be consigned to the
infernal flames or did they go into some sort of hibernation? If the
latter, it could not be a sleep in Christ, since they were already
outside the love of Christ and beyond God's care.

Such were some of the consequences of trying to marry a Greek
immortality theory to a Jewish resurrection one, a doctrine of the
independence of the soul from the body with a doctrine of the unity
of body and soul. The situation was complicated by the fact that
the great medieval schoolmen in the thirteenth century, such as
Thomas Aquinas, having rediscovered Aristotle (then the symbol
of 'secular' philosophy and science), had to try to cope with the fact
that he taught a doctrine of the unity of body and soul that
felicitously fitted the Christian doctrine of resurrection but did not
at all fit the Platonic and Neoplatonic ways of thought that
the Church had used for centuries to express its faith in intellectual
terms. Aristotle's teaching at this point was a godsend in
supporting a resurrection doctrine, which was at the heart of the
Church's official teaching, so on that score he was easily baptized
for the service of the Church. His support, however, aggravated

the long-standing confusion between the notion of a resurrection
that is an award, as in Paul's teaching, and an immortality that is
inalienable, as in the Platonic teaching that Gentile Christianity
had used as its own way of expressing the biblical message in
Gentile terms.

Those who, as a result of the discrediting of the doctrine of
Purgatory at the Reformation, denounced the practice of prayers
for the dead had no less hard a furrow to hoe. Children were
customarily taught that a beloved aunt or grandmother, when she
died, went straight to heaven. What then, became of the doctrine
of resurrection? If she could enjoy the heavenly bliss without a
body, what need could she have of a body, however glorified, after
the Last Trump on the Day of Judgment? If she received a
temporary body, surely it must be one as glorified as would fulfil
the New Testament promise, so why should she exchange it for
another on that day? The notion of the blessed in heaven and the
denizens of hell all assembling for the final sentence of the divine
Court was not merely too legalistic an image; it was ludicrous. Nor
did the interpretations of the learned (who perceived hell as
essentially the pain of the eternal loss of God and heaven as the
enjoyment of the eternal vision of him) diminish the absurdities,
for the concept of resurrection of the body has always been taken
seriously by orthodox Christians, learned or simple.

A further confusion attended the notion of eternality. Was the
life of the world to come one of infinite duration or was it beyond
time and therefore in a different order? The medieval schoolmen
distinguished between *aeternitas*, eternity, and *aeviternitas*,
infinite time. In the Latin Church the phrase *vita aeterna* had
been used traditionally. It is used, for instance, in the Latin version
of the so-called Apostles' Creed and in the Vulgate, in which the
rich man asks Jesus: What should I do *ut vitam aeternam per-
cipiam?*[16] The *eis aiōna* of the New Testament writers however,
like our 'for ever', is used in innocence of this kind of philosophical
distinction. The life promised, the life pertaining to 'the world to
come', is richer, fuller, everlasting life, but whether it is beyond
time or infinite in time is not specified. We ought to be careful not
to read into such phrases what they were not intended to imply and
not to make distinctions that were not clearly envisaged.

The concept of the life of the world to come that is presented to
us in early Christian literature is open to a variety of interpretations. It does not exclude, for example, a continuing process

such as is to be found in a developed reincarnationist view. Surely my life now is richer and fuller than was that of my simian and still earlier ancestors; but it is certainly not as full or as rich as it might be and the promise that it is to be enhanced in richness and fullness in 'the world to come' is of the greatest possible interest to me. That the process should be gradual is as I am disposed to expect as a fulfilment of that promise. As more than one churchgoer has said to me, 'I do not feel ready for heaven'. That is not to deny that we might make tremendous leaps. Such leaps occur in the evolution-ary process. The leap to self-awareness, for example, was a giant step in our past ancestry. Even greater leaps may lie ahead of me, leaps made possible by the work of Christ for my salvation; but the notion that I can jump from my present stage of development into eternity with God seems unintelligible. It is, moreover, unwarrant-ed in Scripture or in early Christian literature, which was content to encourage us to walk in faith into the life beyond. 'To be with Christ . . . is far better.'[17] Need it exclude further pilgrimages that would take me on closer and closer walks with him? *Can* it, indeed, exclude these?

I have briefly considered some of the difficulties attending the development of the three states traditionally discussed in classical theological treatises. There was, however, a further set of puzzles, for some people seemed to be disqualified for all of these states. Two classes in particular did not seem to fit any of the standard destinations.

First, there were those who, having died before the coming of Christ (such as Amos and Plato), could not qualify for heaven. According to an old belief, Christ descended to Sheol (Hades) and retrieved these, the spirits of the holy men and women of old. This theme was much represented in medieval art as the Descent into Hell, sometimes called, in England, the Harrowing of Hell. What precisely happened to them after their retrieval was not clear, but according to the medieval schoolmen (echoed by Dante) they could never attain the perfect vision of God, which is a 'supernatural' enjoyment. Nevertheless, they were destined to unending 'natural' bliss in a state called limbo, the *limbus patrum*. The consequences of this view did not seem to trouble the medieval mind as it would ours. For instance, if I attained heaven I could hope to participate in the Beatific Vision of God along with the rest of redeemed Christians; but, while that would include all sorts of Christians who had scraped by as a result of God's abundant grace for sinners, it could not but exclude Moses and Elijah, Plato and Aristotle, who, though assured of a happy existence for ever, would lack the capacity to share with me in my kind of everlasting bliss. I could never in the life to come meet on the same terms the good men and women who had predeceased Christ.

Second, there was the problem of those infants and others who died before receiving Baptism. What happened to them? For many a mother, not least in medieval and Reformation times, this was a poignant question. Was her little baby whom she so dearly loved to be for ever excluded from heaven because for one reason or another he or she had not received the sacrament of Baptism, which was necessary to wipe out the stain of original sin? Traditionally, the Church assured such mothers that the child would not go to hell; nevertheless, no passage to heaven would ever be possible. The child would go to the *limbus infantium*, the limbo of infants, where it would enjoy happiness but not the bliss of heaven. The same or a similar difficulty arose with respect to those who lived good and holy lives but never had the opportunity of receiving Christian Baptism. Today, moreover, one would have to ask whether we are to suppose that all the great Quaker saints and all the fine Salvationists who have worked so hard for the cause of Christ are to be excluded from heaven and granted only a place in limbo, since neither of these Christian bodies includes Baptism in its practice.

The concept of *limbo*, whether the *limbus patrum* or the *limbus infantium*, presents us with a new puzzle in addition to its aggravation of the confusion already considered. For apart from the appalling injustice that many would see in it, it confronts us in a new way with the question of resurrection. If those in limbo do not get bodies, then it is apparently possible to do without bodies of any kind on a permanent basis, and if they do receive bodies, why cannot these bodies, being presumably glorified, enable them to participate in the joy of heaven? Are we to suppose that their bodies are not glorified enough? If so, is there no way by which they may be developed into the state of glorification necessary for the heavenly bliss? Apparently not, for limbo is a permanent state, not an intermediate one, as is purgatory; it is not a state leading to final bliss.

The character of early Christian discussion of the difference and similarity between resurrection and reincarnation might be variously illustrated and we must give some attention to it in later chapters. For the moment, one example will show what the confusion that was developed so early in Christian thought could lead to even in one of the most interesting, original, and perceptive of the Greek Fathers. Gregory of Nyssa, the fourth-century Cappadocian, perspicaciously notes that those who take a reincarnationist view are 'to a certain extent in accord with the doctrine of the resurrection. Their statement, for example, that the soul after its being released from this body introduces itself into certain other bodies is not absolutely out of harmony with the revival that we are hoping for.' (As I have already suggested, resurrection is a *kind* of reincarnation.) Gregory goes on, however, to specify the difference as he sees it. First he says that all agree that bodies are composed of atoms and he affirms that it is indeed impossible even to imagine a body not composed of such atoms. Then he goes on to say that while reincarnationists suppose that 'the soul alights on other bodies', those who hold a resurrection view contend that 'the same body as before, composed of the same atoms, is compacted around the soul.'[18]

We have no need to fault Gregory for his understanding of the body as a collection of atoms. That accorded with the physics of his day. The notion that the old atoms gather round the soul to yield the resurrected body was, moreover, a way of understanding the process. Some ecclesiastical assemblies have in fact insisted on this. For example, according to the first canon of the Fourth Lateran Council, held in 1215, both the elect and the reprobate are to arise in their own bodies, the bodies that they now have (*omnes cum suis propriis resurgent corporibus, quae nunc gestant*), to receive their reward: unending punishment with the Devil, in the one case, and eternal glory with Christ, in the other. This pronouncement was made no doubt with the Albigensians particularly in view: reincarnation was one of their special tenets. What seems to be overlooked by Gregory and others is that some kind of view has been already presupposed that sees the soul as independent of the body, for it is presented as an entity which on the one view seeks a new body to enter and on the other is clothed anew with the atoms that composed the original body, atoms that have been presumably in some way cleansed and illumined to produce the glorified body that is the Pauline promise. The Pauline doctrine of transformation had been (no doubt unwittingly) itself transformed into a doctrine of re-animation.

Tatian, in the second century, had written that even though fire should destroy every trace of his flesh, the world would receive 'the vaporised matter' which would be stored by God and restored by him to 'its pristine condition'.[19] Here a further development had been already introduced, compounding the earliest confusions: resurrection has now come to be seen as a destiny exemplified by the resurrection of Christ rather than as a hope made possible by Christ's unique miraculous resurrection. Nor need we chide the Christian Apologists and Church Fathers for reading into the New Testament documents what was not there; the Jews who by the time of Jesus believed in resurrection could have found little warrant in the ancient Hebrew Scriptures for their belief, which had been no less an import from extraneous sources. By the time of the Fourth Lateran Council the chaos of belief about the future life had hardened into a crass materialism.

Papias (*c.* AD 60-130), according to Eusebius, adhered to a view expressed by the author of the Apocalypse[20] that there was to be a millenium when the righteous who had died would reign under their Messiah and King for a thousand years. Justin (*c.* 100-*c.*165) also held such a view. The souls of the righteous, he tells us, remain in a better place, the wicked in a worse one, all awaiting the final judgement.[21] Justin acknowledged, however, that many devout Christians of his time thought otherwise.[22] As with so much else in that early period, such a belief represented an option. It also represented, however, the beginnings of a doctrine of the intermediate state, which, though later on hardened into a crude theory of 'temporary punishment', opened the way to a more intelligible and enlighted understanding of the destiny of humankind that was, to say the least, no more unwarranted in Scripture than any of the others. It was, moreover, one that fits well with the reincarnationist option, as we shall see in a later chapter of the present book.

3 Ways of Understanding the Concept of Reincarnation

Under the term *Wiedermenschwerdung*, metempsychosis, or the transmigration of souls, a great variety of ideas may be understood.
Désiré Joseph Mercier, Cardinal Archbishop, *Psychologie*

Before we consider the possibility that a form of reincarnationism
might be compatible with Christian faith and examine such
warrants as we may find in the New Testament and patristic
writings, we must first inspect more carefully what the notion of
reincarnation may mean. We shall find that its meanings are as
varied as are the meanings that have been attached to the notion of
immortality. So we need to clear this ground in order to determine
what form or forms of reincarnationism, if any, might possibly fit a
genuinely Christian mould of thought and which must be ruled
out.

It will be convenient also to discuss at this stage why the concept
of reincarnation should be seriously entertained by Christians at
all. To some who are already for one reason or another favourably
disposed to the idea in principle such a discussion may seem
needless. I hope they will nevertheless bear with it, not only because it is intrinsically important but also because many Christians
do not come to an inquiry such as this with any such initial
predisposition. While some find reincarnational notions inherent-
ly so plausible that they cannot easily set them aside, whatever the
Bible or the Church may say or seem to say about them, others
have not been affected by their power. Over some of us reincarnationism exercises an overwhelmingly persuasive influence; to
others among us it remains merely a weird idea. The first are
inclined to ask: 'Why waste time on what is so obvious? Why not
proceed at once to an examination of the evidence in hope of being
able ot find suport in the proper places for what we simply cannot
help believing?' The second group, however, deserve to be shown

the immensity of the appeal of reincarnationist ideas. Then we may all attend to the specifically Christian question: 'Must an honest Christian who holds such notions renounce them, or may he or she use them to provide a more intelligible Christian hope or at least a viable option to the existing confusion?'

We ask first, then, wherein lies the attraction? To many of us it seems morally preferable to hope that wrongs will be righted in the long run through the operation of a universal moral law in the universe rather than through a judicial assembly with Jesus Christ sitting on the Bench. Such an operation of a moral law does not by any means exclude the operation of divine mercy such as is at the heart of the Gospel message; but neither justice nor mercy should be seen as proceedings in a court, whether of common law or of equity, but rather should be seen as the consequences of our all being, along with the universe itself, in the hands of One from whom all justice and mercy flow. We are too much inclined to see justice and mercy as antithetical and therefore to marvel at the paradox of a just God who can also be merciful when he so pleases. To think like this is, however, to betray a spiritual immaturity that restricts both God's justice and his mercy to our human limits. If God is as the New Testament writers say, then his justice must pervade every action that is ever performed, bringing the strict consequences of it with inexorable certainty and often with much pain, while at the same time God's overwhelming love and care, his 'amazing grace', sweeps through these moral consequences. It is at this that Shakespeare hints in *The Merchant of Venice* when he calls the quality of mercy 'not strain'd' and pronounces it 'an attribute to God himself.'[1] If there be any mercy in God at all, it must surely permeate the divine justice. God's mercy must be dyed in the wool of his justice and his justice dyed in the wool of his mercy.

The effects of the moral law may come quickly, as do often those of physical laws. The apple ripens; it falls to the ground. One over-indulges at the office party; next morning, the 'punishment' is a hangover. Often, however, physical effects take a very long time to show. The effects of excessive radiation, for instance, may show up for the first time fifty years later in a cancer. Light from another star, despite its high velocity, takes years to reach us. So with the moral law. Its effects show up sometimes at once sometimes in a few years; but often they do not catch up with the perpetrator of cruelty or injustice during his or her entire lifetime.

On a reincarnational view they do catch up with the perpetrator sooner or later: perhaps in the next lifetime, perhaps only after many lifetimes. Meanwhile the wicked prosper and the righteous groan. Nor does grace obliterate the wrongs. Grace is not a cosmic free lunch. What it does is to make possible the cure of the moral disease, which is surely reason enough to justify a Christian's rejoicing.

In face of such considerations, the appeal of the principle of a cosmic moral law is to many of us overwhelming. Such a law, inseparable from any developed form of reincarnationism, accords with that hope of the triumph of righteousness that is common to both Judaism and Christianity. 'God's law' is then to be seen, not as a merely useful piece of legislation in summary form given to Moses on Mount Sinai for the development of a primitive people, nor even as the first five books of the Bible that Jews revere as the Torah, but as the law that is the nature of God himself, which by no means excludes the grace revealed to us in Jesus Christ, his unique embodiment in human form. If, as the psalmist says, the law of the Lord is perfect, converting the soul,[2] it must surely encompass the mercies of the Lord that the psalmist also praises.[3] As grace presupposes nature,[4] so it must presuppose the law of him who bestows it; hence Jesus's insistence that he did not come to destroy the law but to complete it.[5] Both grace and the moral law are revelations of the nature of God. Far from making God impersonal, what is being proposed here exhibits the truth that the God whom we Christians acclaim as 'the Father of Jesus Christ' must encompass within his nature *at least* those qualities we call 'personal' and specially prize on that account. The fact that in some of the traditions of Indian religious philosophy the moral law or karma may be understood in a way that seems to us impersonal does not mean that that is the only way or even the best way of understanding the moral or karmic law.

Besides the moral appeal of reincarnationism, its consonance with what we now know from the sciences of the evolutionary character of the universe is an immensely persuasive factor. No revolution in the history of western thought has been more far-reaching in its results than the one associated with the recognition that whatever is has come about by an evolutionary process. The discoveries of Darwin and Huxley are only one aspect of a far-reaching principle. Those who see no reason to believe in the kind of God to which Christian experience bears witness will see no reason to go beyond this evolutionary principle; but we who have reason to do so will see evolution as the way of God in accomplishing whatever his ends are. Creation is not achieved by divine wand-waving. It is a costly process: billions of years to bring about even the conditions of life that would make the evolution of humanity possible and millions more and incalculable anguish to accomplish this result. Moreover, according to the most specifically Christian teaching about the love of God, the redemption of humankind is so costly that it entails the Cross, which is to be understood not only as an event on Calvary two thousand years ago but as written into the very nature of God's own being as Creator. It is a divine principle. There are no cosmic free lunches. The reason is simple: love entails sacrifice and the suffering that attends it, and God is love *par excellence*.

When we think along such lines the notion that our moral and spiritual development should entail a long process of evolution seems to many of us so obvious as to need no demonstration. The notion that the struggle we see in the biological realm for the development and survival of the species suggests, along with much else, that in the moral and spiritual realms one must surely expect no less a struggle but, rather, a much greater one. This struggle *could* be understood as an entirely tooth-and-claw affair, much as the biological process was at one time; but it need not be so understood. No more need moral and spiritual evolution be understood exclusively in terms of a might-is-right or will-to-power type of theory than need religion be understood as merely the fear of the unknown, although primitive forms of religion may well begin with this. If we do consent to see evolution as a general principle, as all modern scientific thinking so strongly suggests is the case, does not some kind of reincarnationist principle follow? Surely the working out of our moral and spiritual development must take longer than a few decades of one particular life, hedged about by limiting, not to say imprisoning, circumstances, or (as is often the case) a few weeks or even days. That a Christian's opportunity to grow in grace and progress in wisdom should be so arbitrarily limited seems at best capricious and at worst monstrous. In fact, of course, the notion of an intermediate state (purgatory or whatever it may be called) provides in some vague way for further development. A reincarnational interpretation of the intermediate state as traditionally presented would make that doctrine infinitely more intelligible, much less punitive, and a great deal more consonant with what Christian experience shows us of the workings of God's love and care even as it is revealed to us within the confines of one little human life.

The notion that we reap what we sow is biblical.[6] That we make our own future circumstances is at least a partly undeniable psychological truth, if nothing more. By contrast, the notion that if I can 'get away with murder' I reap no consequences, so that God must come in the end with his avenging sword to punish me for what I was clever enough to do without injuring myself in any way, is to many of us a horrible travesty of God's dealings with his creatures. The notion that in the sight of God there is no second chance even for a murderer is alien to all that the Gospels tell us of God's ways of providing opportunities for forgiveness. Moreover, the gross inequities of the life we know here on earth poses a notoriously intractable problem to all who have ever seriously reflected on the subject, from Job to Augustine, from Boethius to contemporary thinkers. The wicked *do* flourish and the righteous *are* and *remain* the victims of appalling injustice in this life. The concept of reincarnation provides at least a serious proposal of how these inequities could be sorted out in the course of millions, perhaps trillions, of years, if not at the next turn of the wheel of rebirth. On a reincarnationist view we could say that we are each given a task, a mission, to be accomplished. Some succeed and go on to other, higher tasks as does a boy or girl who succeeds at school and goes on to the university. Others try but do not quite finish. Surely God does not shut the door upon them. If even those who administer our scholastic and professional examinations on earth allow us to re-sit, surely the God of love will not deny us a chance to try again when we failed to finish within the time allotted to us, especially since, unlike these examinations, human life is of indeterminable duration.

Those of us who are of an individualistic turn of mind are likely to find reincarnationism an exciting concept if only because it so conspicuously exalts the individual. I am not merely a member of a community; I am an individual with personal awareness and personal responsibility. The classic formulations of most of the major religions of the world (Hinduism, Judaism, Christianity, and Islam) all speak out of a cultural outlook in which the role of the community is overwhelmingly important and the individual comparatively insignificant. In classical Hinduism the significance of blood and soil is difficult to exaggerate. In the religion of the

Hebrew people God spoke through lawgivers and prophets to the people, entering into a covenant with Israel. In Christianity, as classically presented, there is a new covenant, but the concept of the community is still inescapable. The Church is the New Israel. Mohammed, who borrowed many ideas from Jewish and Christian sources, gave his followers a vision of a vast theocratic community. So it had to be, for the notion of the individual as we understand it today is a comparatively modern one. Reincarnationist teachings, however, stress the individual's responsibility above all else.

In those bygone ages only exceptional people had the capacity to transcend that community-oriented mentality; they were men and women of unusual moral awareness and spiritual perceptivity. Nowadays vast numbers of educated people, even those showing little that could be called spirituality or personal holiness, are strongly aware of themselves as individuals and expect the community to subserve the interests and needs of the individuals who compose it. All this suggests, I submit, that reincarnationist ideas, whatever their theological merits or defects, are capable of much wider appeal than could have been the case in the ancient world or even the Middle Ages.

Enough has been said here to suggest at least some of the reasons why reincarnationism, which for millenia has played a remarkable role in the history of religions, has the capacity to feature even more significantly in the thought of men and women today. Its appeal in our age is widely felt. Before we can usefully approach the question whether Christianity can welcome it or must shut its doors upon it, we must now consider, as promised, the diversity of ways in which it can be understood.

Take first a very common and almost universally accepted observation. We all have, each one of us, a biological ancestry. Long before anything was known of genes and other scientific postulates about heredity, people noticed that individual members of a faimily 'took after' this or that ancestor. An observant aunt would remark that not only Mary's features and hair colour clearly resembled those of her grandmother much more than those of her parents; so also did her temperament and her inclinations. Perhaps even a much more unlikely 'throw-back' would be noticed. In some cases the resemblance noted was so overwhelmingly strong that the observer would go so far as to say something such as: 'I am old enough to remember Mary's great-great-grand-mother when she was a very old lady, and this child Mary is so like her that it is as if that old lady has simply taken possession of her. When I look at the way Mary is developing, when I consider her talents and her tantrums, her walk, her speech, her way of turning her head, her ambitions, and her faults, it is the old lady all over again. It's not that Mary is *like* her: Mary *is* she.'

Now, of course not everybody who has talked like that has had reincarnational notions in mind. Many probably have never heard of the notion. Moreover, many reincarnationists would not call that reincarnation at all. Nevertheless, I think it may be called a *form* of it. It is a corollary of the widespread notion that we achieve a sort of immortality by having children. I may be said 'to live on' in my son or daughter and so through all the generations to come. Hence at least one of the reasons for the widespread sense of the importance or desirability of having children to carry on one's line. Of course men with large estates are likely to be gratified by the prospect that they should be inherited by their descendants; but on this type of immortality theory even the poorest man on earth may feel assured of a far grander prospect: his heirs of line will inherit himself. As we might say, his blood will flow in their veins long after his corpse has rotted in the grave. If his blood can be so reincarnated, then so also can the other constituents of his body. His wife shares with him this hope of immortality, for they have contributed equally to the process of what we may call reincarnation by heredity.

Nor is such an immortality merely the perpetuation of the parents' physical qualities or endowments. If (as is widely held) mind and body, whatever they are, are inseparable, then our minds, our souls, our spirits, no less than our bodies, must be reincarnated in our descendants too. Jung's theory of a collective unconscious or race unconscious would seem, then, to be less fantastic than at first it might have appeared, for the less speculative theory of transmission of qualities through genes gives it plausibility. Through a line of carriers of qualities and endowments, physical and mental, I have inherited whatever I started out with in my mother's womb. These are my genetic circumstances.

Suppose that, as has indeed occurred, a mental prodigy issues from the most unlikely parents. I remember hearing, for instance, of a boy of seven who was clearly a musical genius of the highest order. The musical capacity of his parents, who were coarse and unlettered folk, was limited to singing *Clementine* and the like off key around a camp fire. Whence did the boy receive his astounding musical talent? There was no vestige of it to be found in the boy's ancestry for several generations back. But then even the most genealogically-conscious families are seldom able to show a *complete* ancestral record beyond a few generations. The reason is that we have too many ancestors. The genetic pool is incalculably large. Most of us can identify, beyond our two parents and our four grandparents, probably most of our eight great-grandparents and perhaps even most of our sixteen great-great-grandparents. These sixteen direct ancestors of mine, however, had among them four generations further back no fewer than 256 great-great-grandparents, all to be reckoned in my genetic pool. As we go back in four-generation jumps the figures soon become astronomical. For these 256 had 4096; these in turn had 65 536; these 1 048 576; and these 16 777 216. If we take a generation to be 25 years, that hardly takes us back to the age of Chaucer, a small span indeed in human history. Go only six or seven generations further back still, which would not take us even to Thomas à Becket, and the corresponding figure would be theoretically over a billion! Inbreeding, of course, explains the otherwise impossible figures. The point I am making is that by any reckoning we draw from such an incalculably enormous genetic pool that one might plausibly argue that it could account for the phenomena to which proponents of traditional reincarnationist teaching point as demanding the type of explanation they offer.

According to more classical types of reincarnationist teaching, the reason for my possession of certain qualities and dispositions must be sought beyond the generally accepted principles of genetics. They are to be found, they say, in my having acquired or attained them in previous lives. We ought to take very seriously, however, the possibility that they are the result of the vast complexities of the genetic process. That Mozart or some such musical genius has been reincarnated in a contemporary child prodigy born of oafish parents and into a dull, unimaginative family is a fascinating speculation, perhaps; but is it necessary? Is not the genetic one more probable? Experiments with fruit flies, which reproduce so rapidly that they are particularly well adapted to genetic research, have demonstrated that certain characteristics do not show till certain pairs are crossed. I understand that breeders of race horses and prize cattle keep computer records, nowadays, of the desirable and undesirable qualities and that they succeed to a remarkable extent in conserving the former and eliminating the latter.

Whether mental and spiritual qualities can be so bred is, however, much less clear. Perhaps a combination of genetic traits might issue in a facility in languages or a skill in mathematics; but is there a combination that produces heroic courage, penetrating psychological insight, or acute reasoning powers? What sort of combination of genes would produce a singular talent for Sanskrit in a person not otherwise notably gifted in languages? The colour and texture of my hair are presumably derived from the genetic pool, and whence I acquired such physical traits is often quite obvious; but can everything that goes into my uniqueness as an individual be explained by heredity? Were Hitler and Schweitzer both merely the result of chance genetic combinations, the one unfortunate and the other felicitous? In view of the enormous magnitude of the genetic pool and the way heredity works, the genetic hypothesis is not to be entirely discarded out of hand. Nevertheless, does not it seem more likely that genetic explanations and Jung's theory of the collective unconscious provide at most only a part of the explanation we seek?

We turn, therefore, to another line of inquiry: the one suggested in the ancient philosophical tradition, to which Christianity, as we have seen, has not been entirely unindebted. According to this ancient wisdom, I do inherit much from my biological ancestors (no doubt much more than the colour of my hair and the set of my jaw); nevertheless, what is really most distinctive and important about me is not hereditary at all. It is the result of how I have worked out tasks allotted to me in previous lives. On this theory, which is basically common to both the Upanishads and Plato (who received it in its Pythagorean form), the fundamental 'I' transcends not only my body but what is customarily understood by my 'soul' or 'mind', since even these are but its temporary clothing. What I receive through my heredity is by no means unimportant. (Plato believed much in it.) On the contrary, it is central to the circumstances with which I have to deal. My heredity is by far the most important aspect of my environment. I choose my heredity as one chooses (at least ideally) one's school or one's teacher. When I pass through this life I enter into a different dimension of being. Then, perhaps very soon or perhaps not for centuries (according to our reckoning on planet Earth), I recognize the need to enter into a new womb. I need the new experience for my further development. I may be very advanced and yet make what is by conventional human standards a poor choice (for example, to be the crippled son or daughter of an illiterate peasant), since that is what seems needed for the particular kind of spiritual advancement I have to make. Or I may be very unadvanced and yet succeed in selecting the womb of a gifted princess and be born, as the world will say, with a silver spoon in my mouth, because that happens to be what I need for my development, at that particular stage. It is what is dictated by my total moral circumstances under the karmic law.

In point of fact, in the brahminical tradition in India, which developed the caste system, the two ideas were held together: one was born into a lower caste till one had achieved what was necessary for birth into a higher. Buddhism was, besides much else, a protest against the traditional brahminical view. According to Buddhist principles, one could never tell from social and institutional circumstances such as caste what was the real state of anyone's spiritual attainment. If, however, both a genetic and an upanishadic option were viable in terms of Christian faith and contemporary scientific thought, we might use both. Let us first glance, however, at what the upanishadic type of theory, which is substantially of the type that Plato seems to have inherited from Pythagoras, entails.

The underlying presupposition of such a reincarnational theory is that not only the physical, flesh-and-bones body, but any other 'subtler' bodies that we may inhabit, are mere clothes that we assume for temporary periods in the course of our long pilgrimage. The inmost self that passes through these various habitations is independent not only of our flesh-and-bones body but of 'astral' bodies and other bodies that may clothe us along the way. At death I cast off the outer shell that is my corpse, but even the finer body that is a sort of double is by no means the real 'me'. To get to the real 'me' I must go through a process of stripping till I reach the naked self. It is this naked self that is reincarnated. It transcends not only the particular body I now inhabit, which happens to be white and male, with predominantly Scottish genes and in excellent health, but also my mind, for whatever it is worth, and my distinctive personality which I so much associate (as do my friends) with the real 'me'. My mind and my personality, however, are almost as ephemeral as my flesh-and-bones body. In the long run they have little more to do with the real 'me' than has the pin-stripe suit I happen to be wearing this season. In the vague sense in which perhaps one might say that my brain has more to do with the real me than has my big toe, perhaps my personality with its distinctive traits might be said to have more to do with me than has my skin, but when we look at all these matters from a long-range perspective, skin, brain, personality and bone-marrow are all but clothing.

So far, such a view might not be entirely unadaptable to Christian baptism, some difficulties notwithstanding. On the typical Buddhist theories, however, even the 'me' itself eventually evaporates, at least in the sense that *Nibbāna* is an experience in which the notion of 'I' and 'me' disappears.[7] There is indeed a place for the concept of self-negation in Christian experience, but the sense of individuality is so strong in Christian faith and Christian thought that its undercutting always poses special problems, to say the least, in any Christian programme of salvation. Still, the whole concept of salvation by means of a long series of pilgrimages through temporary circumstances that do not constitute my real home is eminently consonant with the Christian understanding of what we are doing here on earth, where, Scripture tells us, 'we have no permanent home, but we are seekers after the city which is to come.'[8]

There is no doubt that a view of the self or soul in that general Platonic tradition has been enormously influential in the development of Christian thought, however much or little it may be deemed to accord with the central New Testament witness. Some of the most characteristic Christian teachings seem to suggest that the soul or self is detachable as well as all-important. 'What does a man gain', asks Jesus, 'by winning the whole world at the cost of his true self? What can he give to buy that self back?'[9] Jesus, on the cross, 'yielded up the ghost'.[10] According to traditional Catholic teaching, certain sins 'kill the soul'. The gravamen of practically all medieval Christian teaching was that the body is a mere instrument at best, and at the worst an obstacle, in the soul's march toward the promised land. That very Platonic view, which permeated all medieval thought, the later medieval challenge of Aristotle notwithstanding, was certainly not set aside in Renaissance thought; on the contrary, it was reinforced by the discovery of the humanistic sources. Pico della Mirandola taught that the soul passes out of one body and enters another. As G.F. Moore remarked in his Ingersoll Lecture at Harvard, it is not surprising that with the revival of Platonism and Plotinianism at the Renaissance 'the theory of metempsychosis was revived in European philosophy.'[11] Neither Plato nor Plotinus had really needed reviving in the Middle Ages, however, for medieval thought was saturated with their presuppositions; the Renaissance merely provided a better literary methodology, a surer way of getting to the original sources, unencumbered by stultifying 'authorities'. Nineteenth-century English Protestant literature remained saturated with the notion that on the Christian view the soul is what counts; the body, valuable a tool though it be, is no more than a tool. We shall have an opportunity later of seeing much more of this type of influence in western literature.

Having looked at two basic types of immortality theory, both susceptible to reincarnational treatment, we have found nothing in either of them that is intrinsically incompatible with Christian faith. That is far from saying, of course, that we have so far found any reason for adopting either of them. The first of the views we have examined is probably in fact held, in one way or another, by many scientifically-minded Christians who would not normally think of it as a reincarnationist view at all. The second view, provided that we do not introduce into it the specifically pantheistic notions that generally accompany it in its oriental forms, is much more in line with what is commonly understood when we talk of reincarnational ideas, at any rate at any level beyond the primitive, magical kinds with which we are not concerned here. It preserves a sense of the growth and development of the individual and of the intensification of his or her self-awareness that are such typical constituents of the thought and language of Christian writers from early times, especially in the mystical traditions that have flowered in Christian soil. All of these, from the cautious Benedictine mysticism to be found in Gregory the Great and Bernard of Clairvaux, for example, to the more colourful Spanish types, and from Augustine's to the French Salesian tradition, as well as mystical outlooks that are specifically within the Reformation heritage, seem to presuppose the loneliness of the soul in its quest for God, its joy in attaining union with him, and an intensified self-awareness as union with God is achieved. For their presuppositions owe much, however indirectly, to the Platonic and Neoplatonic moulds of thought out of which so much of Christian thought has been constructed.

There are two principal types of objection to this second

immortality theory found in Christian thought, the one objection of a very different kind from the other.

The first objection is the philosophical and scientific one arising from considerations of the mind-body problem. These considerations are much too complex to be discussed at this stage. We shall deal with that problem later on. We note for the moment only that the notion of a 'soul' as an independent entity, capable of existing apart from a body, though finding a body for one reason or another a convenient instrument for the soul's development, is radically alien to all that we know of human consciousness. I can and do transcend my animal nature, but no matter how far I travel beyond it I never cease to be attached to my body; I can never dispense with it. I may severely discipline it, if I am of an ascetic disposition, but I cannot do without it. Furthermore, I cannot imagine what it would be like to have no body at all. I can imagine quite easily having a different kind of body, but to be a disembodied spirit seems inconceivable. [12] My memory for instance, seems to be entirely dependent on my brain cells. When these are seriously injured or fail to make the necessary 'telephone connections', I become unable to recall. These are among the more obvious considerations to which we must attend later.

The other principal objection is, rather, a biblical and theological one. As Oscar Cullmann and others have pointed out, the most characteristic form of the Christian hope as presented in the New Testament is not a theory of immortality such as Plato's but a doctrine of resurrection. Resurrection is at the very core of the apostolic *kerygma*, the proclamation of the Good News about Jesus Christ. Because he has risen, we can hope to rise too and receive a new and better body. The New Testament writers were to some extent prepared for this concept by certain trends in late pre-Christian Jewish thought, which included, as we have noted in an earlier chapter, a concept of resurrection. The New Testament writers were distinctly Jewish in their thought-patterns, however much the Jewishness of these thought-patterns had been affected by Hellenistic ideas. The Christian hope they hold out to us is of resurrection to new life.

Generally speaking, resurrection was an idea that struck the Greek mind as absurd. Augustine remarks that the Greeks, while they were open to the concept of the immortality of the soul, accounted that of resurrection totally impossible. [13] They were thinking of it as an ascent of the flesh-and-bones body up to heaven, which not unnaturally they accounted absurd. In fact, however, the early Christian writers, including Paul himself, by no means clearly specify the meaning of the resurrection for which we are to hope. True, it is certainly not transmigration from one body to another that has nothing to do with the first. It is a rising with a new and 'glorified' body. Yet not only is the nature of the body unspecified; Paul positively discourages speculations on that subject.[14] He does, however, provide a clue: *each sort of seed gets its own sort of body.*[15] That is a notion that is very compatible with a reincarnational understanding of human destiny, which is not to say, of course, that Paul taught reincarnationism of the upanishadic or Platonic type. It may be, nevertheless, that we should not exclude that hypothesis. As we shall see later, several of the Christian Fathers note the similarity between resurrection and transmigration.

Resurrection is certainly a *kind* of reincarnation, however much we care to outlaw Platonic forms of the latter and insist that resurrection is a form of reincarnation that is by no means to be classed with other kinds. For if I am supposed to shed my body and assume or receive it back in a superior form, we cannot deny that I have lost my old body and acquired a new one. That is surely to have migrated from one body to another. The second body may stand in the same relation to 'me' as did the first, whatever that relation be, but all the language about resurrection seems to presuppose my taking possession of another and better body.

Of course one might point out that a child grows out of its body and into an adult one at puberty and through adolescence, yet we recognize that it is 'the same' body. We recognize that we are constantly renewing the cells of our bodies and repairing slight injuries that we incur from day to day, yet we certainly do not talk of getting new bodies in such a context. Resurrection seems to presuppose that the organization of my body (*sōma*) is not fundamentally changed: I am to stand in the same relation to my new body, whatever form it may take, as I stand to my present body. That, however, is just the sort of presupposition that the proponents of the Platonic type of immortality theory make about me and the bodies I successively inhabit.

After all, even though we were to accept the notion (something of a caricature) that according to the Platonic and upanishadic forms of reincarnationism the body is to be regarded as a mere suit of clothes, we must surely recognize that even a suit of clothes must 'fit' the person. So of course so long as the body is in any way seen as standing in relation to a 'me', it must somehow fit me. The resurrection teaching seems to be, indeed, that as I grow in grace and am raised by Christ to higher things, the glorified body that is promised me is one that will fit my enhanced state. That, too, is not at all incompatible with a developed reincarnationist theory. It accords with the general principle of evolution that we find in all things. The body of a turtle is adapted to its state of being. With evolutionary advance it ceases to be a fitting body. As we advance, the chemistry of our bodies may become eventually unsuited to our enhanced state of being and we shall move to another kind of embodiment, possibly on another planet; but meanwhile, not being ready for that leap, we may pass through some more incarnations in the present type of body, the sort of body to which we are now accustomed.

Since we are soon to be confronted with references to reincarnationist ideas as they occur in various historical and contemporary contexts, this is a convenient place to note certain matters of usage. Most scholars today use four terms synonymously: 'rebirth', 'transmigration', 'reincarnation', and 'metempsychosis', for in the history of ideas they seem to have been used indifferently. When Hume, in the eighteenth century, for example, uses the term 'metempsychosis', he does not seem to be intending anything different from what other western philosophers have generally intended by the term 'transmigration'. He is merely adopting the Greek form and they the Latin. The terms 'reincarnation' and 'rebirth' are likewise used by most writers indiscriminately. All such terms may be used in relation to either the most primitive or the most highly developed and ethical forms of the notion. We should note, however, that certain groups do make distinctions of their own. In modern theosophical circles, for instance, the term 'transmigration' is usually pre-empted to signify the primitive form and 'reincarnation' preferred in allusion to the developed, ethical form of the doctrine.

Certain other terms have been used, however, with a more specialized intent. The term 'metensomatosis', as used by some of the early Christian Fathers, does seem to intend at least a special emphasis: not the migration of the *psychē* from one body to another but, rather, the fresh organization of the *sōma*, the body conceived as an organizing principle. The term 'palingenesis', much used by Polish and other writers in the nineteenth century, may also be invested with special meanings. In general, however, we should look to ambiguities in the reincarnational idea itself rather than to the notion of a distinguishing terminology, for most of the ambiguities have been unconsciously introduced and the terminology largely accidental.

In showing something of the variety of presuppositions that can underlie reincarnational notions, my purpose has not been, of course, merely to provide materials for a comparative study. Even less has it been to try to exhibit an exhaustive list of the possibilities, were that feasible. My aim has been more fundamental: to show that, whatever judgment one eventually makes on any proposal to accept a reincarnational account of the destiny of humankind, one must be careful not to base that judgment on one particular form of reincarnationism to the exclusion of other possibilities. The concept is detachable from the various presuppositions to which it has been anchored in the history of ideas. We ought no more to feel constrained to accept a Pythagorean form of reincarnationism, with all its metaphysical implications, and to sneak it somehow into the mainstream of Christian thought, than we need feel forced to recognize an ancient Babylonian cosmology and to squeeze it into the Christian catechism. By the same token, we ought not to discard what we take to be important spiritual truth merely because it seems vitiated by attachment to outmoded theories or polluted by association with wrongheaded or ignorant assumptions. To do so is to end by renouncing all the wisdom of the ages, since all of it has been necessarily formulated according to intellectual models that in the nature of the case cannot be expected to remain for ever viable.

I have tried to show, therefore, that we should consider the merits of the concept of reincarnation as a Christian hope without allowing any such prejudices to get in the way of our judgment. Nevertheless, for us Christians, this does not mean that the concept should be accepted merely because it happens to have for us the strong appeal that it has indubitably exercised over thoughtful people for thousands of years, both in the East and (as we shall see), to a greater extent than many suppose, also in the West. We must try to see how thoughtful Christians, especially in the early centuries of the Christian Way, have regarded it, and with that in view let us now turn our attention to such biblical and patristic witness as we can find.

4 New Testament and Patristic Witness

Rabbi, who sinned, this man or his parents? Why was he born blind?
John 9.2 (NEB)

When a thoughtful Christian approaches the New Testament, he
or she enters upon very special terrain. For the New Testament is
acclaimed by the Church as part of canonical Scripture. It is not
like other literature as something that one can take or leave. I may
account Pascal the greatest of all Christian writers and affirm that
it was he who brought me to Christ, while you may say (and are
perfectly entitled to say) that you have never been able to see much
in him. None of us, however, may so treat the Bible, for its
documents are the primary witnesses of the Christian faith. Nevertheless, how we approach the Bible is another and by no means
uncontroversial question. The Bible is a complex literature.[1]
The words of the New Testament must be interpreted in the light
of all our knowledge if we are to do justice to the revelation we
acclaim in it. Yet 'the word of our God shall stand for ever'.[2]

The significance of these remarks for our present purpose is
plain. We must not ask questions such as: 'Does the New
Testament teach reincarnation or not? If it does, where is the text?
If it does not, how dare we encourage a plainly unbiblical
doctrine?' That is a radically wrong approach. If we were to use it
we would obscure truth rather than display it. We must try to see,
rather, whether reincarnation is or is not the sort of doctrine that
would have been in the minds of the biblical writers and then see,
so far as we can, what sort of attitude they would have taken
towards it. In short, their witness need not be expressed in a
specific text. We have already noted in an earlier chapter that the
doctrine of the Trinity, for example, is not expressed in such a text.

According to John the Evangelist, when the disciples encountered a man blind from his birth, they asked their Master a very
particular question: 'Rabbi, who sinned, this man or his parents?
Why was he born blind?'[3] Apparently the disciples felt there had to
be an explanation. Here was a seeming injustice of the first order: a
man who was blind, not because of any misfortune that had
happened to him in the course of the vicissitudes of life, but
congenitally. We are led to suppose that they entertained two
possibilities: (1) his parents or other ancestors had sinned and had
transmitted the consequences of their sin to the poor child in the
form of congenital blindness, or (2) the man himself, before his
birth, had sinned in some way that had resulted in this terrible
misfortune. If the second alternative is to be seriously entertained,
it must be seen as presupposing a previous life or lives in which the
sin had occurred, with these horrible consequences, for there is no
other way in which a new-born child could conceivably be
supposed to have sinned, unless in the womb, which is absurd.

The recorded response of Jesus to the question is clear: the man
was born blind 'that God's power might be displayed in curing
him.'[4] Jesus then proceeds to the demonstration of that divine
power, which he has authority to exercise. He spits on the ground,
makes a paste of the spittle, spreads it on the man's eyes, tells him
to go and wash in the pool of Siloam, and the man returns, able to
see.[5]

So far as the Gospel record goes, Jesus ignores the reincarnational implications of the question, which are striking. He is
depicted as unwilling to endorse either of the alternatives with
which the disciples confront him. He affirms that the man was
born blind for the express purpose of providing a demonstration of
the divine power. The disciples, however, have raised a general
question concerning what would nowadays be called the problem
of evil, which Jesus is represented as simply choosing not to treat
here, in the context they have given. That the disciples had a
reincarnational hypothesis in mind is nevertheless plain enough;
nor is it astonishing that they should have been thinking along such
lines, and that the Evangelist should have noted their interest in
such ideas, since reincarnation was one of the many ideas
circulating in that clearing house of religious patterns of thought
that was the Mediterranean world of the time. The disciples were
plainly concerned with the old problem: we seem to start life with
inequities and finish it with inequities; how can this be squared

with the justice of God whose Kingdom is coming, being even already on its way?

The prophet Malachi, who was writing sometime after the rebuilding of the Temple in 516 BC and before certain reforms that were introduced by the year 432 BC, had announced: 'Look, I will send you the prophet Elijah before the great and terrible day of the Lord comes.'[6] Matthew refers three times to this prophecy and the other Evangelists also allude to it. The disciples, like other Jews of the time, showed much interest in it. After the mysterious episode celebrated in Christian tradition as the Transfiguration, in the course of which the disciples saw Moses and Elijah conversing with their Master, they are reported by Matthew as having asked Jesus why the scribal authorities say that Elijah must come first. To this Jesus replies that Elijah has come already and that the people had 'failed to recognize him'. Matthew goes on: 'Then the disciples understood that he meant John the Baptist'.[7] When Jesus, on another occasion, asked his disciples who people said he was, they replied: 'Some say John the Baptist, others Elijah, others Jeremiah, or one of the prophets.' [8]

Whatever we may take Jesus's own teaching to be on the subject of reincarnation, it is clear that the notion was in the minds of the disciples and of other thoughtful people of the time. Some read into the words of Jesus in this connection ('If you have ears that can hear, then hear'[9] a positive esoteric teaching of this kind; but at any rate the notion was in the air. The priests asked John the Baptist directly: 'Are you Elijah?'[10] According to Luke, when Herod heard of the doings of Jesus, he did not know what to make of it all. Some 'were saying that John had been raised from the dead, others that Elijah had appeared, others again that one of the old prophets had come back to life.'[11] These are certainly not questions that the average churchgoer today would be likely to raise concerning a great saint or teacher that appeared on the horizon and was the talk of the town. They are, however, characteristic of the way people were thinking at the time of Jesus.

Let us be particularly careful not to conclude rashly from texts such as these that 'the Bible teaches' reincarnationism. Before we go any further we must be very clear on a basic point that I find crucially important. The biblical writers tell us, each in his own way, joyful news of God's dealings with and attitude toward us human beings and of how we can be saved from final destruction. They do not teach specific metaphysical doctrines or insist on making this or that ontological claim. Mixed with the Good News they tell, we find, of course, certain attitudes of mind inseparable from metaphysical and ontological presuppositions that they unconsciously hold or that come naturally to them in their circumstances. To what extent such metaphysical accompaniments are important and to what extent they are expendable is an extremely complex and difficult question in biblical and indeed in all literary criticism. In the earlier part of the thousand-year period in which the Bible was written the thought-patterns and the presuppositions are comparatively simple, not to say primitive. Indeed, in their case our major difficulty is getting back to such a simple and uncluttered way of thinking, with the largely uncritical outlook it entailed. In the later books, notably Job, the Wisdom literature, and the New Testament, is to be found an awareness of alternative ways of looking at the mystery of human existence, but little or no methodology adequate for the purpose of preferring one theory over another. Hebrew thought was not on the whole much concerned with philosophical conundrums of that kind.

By New Testament times the Jews had been exposed to some of the fashionable discussions in the Mediterranean world, but comparatively few people, Jewish or Gentile, were equipped to make intelligent choices such as we Christians today might hope to find them making. For this reason we need not expect to find any pronouncement in the Bible on so speculative a question as the transmigration of souls. Even the notion of the soul itself emerges with none of the critical awareness that we expect of scholars today. The Hebrews did not have a *theory* of the unity of body and soul, for example. Such a theory may be said to represent fairly well what they took the situation to be, but they did not have a theory as did Aristotle. The New Testament writers could not have been ignorant of the notion that souls transmigrate; but to pretend that they, or any one of them, championed it or denounced it would be indeed far-fetched, if not absurd. It is not that we find no decision, positive or negative; looking for one would be futile. What I think we do find is that they knew of the idea and that at least some of them were by no means uninterested in it.

At an early stage of the development of Christian literature is to be found, however, a much more radical divergence on a most fundamental matter: the way in which Scripture is to be read. It is a divergence that has continued to plague us all through our history and plagues us still. Two different types of mind-set are represented: one that tends to read everything literally (and therefore also Scripture) and another that tends to see allegory in everything in which allegory could possibly be seen. In the Middle Ages the allegorising tendency became so prevalent that it engendered many fanciful and capricious ideas, thereby provoking demand for correctives, expressed, for instance, by the Victorine school: 'Back to the text!' Nevertheless, there have been many men and women in all ages who have been virtually incapable of seeing beyond 'the letter' to 'the figure' and have read the Bible as though it were a legal document such as a contract of sale or a disposition of property, while others contrive to read into it almost whatever they would like it to say. Few have the discriminating imagination and disciplined creativity to read the text and hear with it the descant of spiritual truths to which no text can ever do more than point the way.

The allegoristic approach is certainly fraught with danger. For creative imagination can easily degenerate into profitless wild fancy. Some aspects of the second-century Christian Gnostic sects provide notorious examples of that wayward tendency. Yet how foolish it is to belittle or condemn all allegorising of Scripture (as is so often done) because much of it has exhibited such pernicious inclinations. As well might one spurn all poetry because many, (probably most), of the world's versifying scribblers have written nothing but triviality and trash. There is no way of understanding any spiritual truth through Scripture that does not entail allegorising of one kind or another. The attempt to read Scripture literalistically can end only in disaster, despair or disgust, for the task is not merely a difficult one; it is radically misconceived. Whether, indeed, it is possible to read anything literally without qualification is a serious philosophical question and one that need not concern us here; but in any case Scripture is not susceptible to any such treatment. If anything in the Bible can be usefully read in this way, it can be only incidental affirmations of no fundamental importance either for one's salvation or for one's better insight into spiritual truths, such as the distance between two cities or a man's age at the time of his death: matters on which the Bible is not always notably accurate and certainly not infallible.

Among the early Fathers, however, we already find representatives of the two tendencies. Tertullian, for example, a Latin-speaking lawyer who was converted to Christianity in the last

decade of the second century, takes a typically literalistic approach
to the biblical passages cited at the beginning of this chapter.
Tertullian is well aware of the transmigrational view and,
although he recognizes that it is a belief that 'most nearly
approaches' the accepted doctrine of the resurrection of the
body,[12] he shows no sympathy towards it.

Tertullian devotes considerable space to refuting the transmigrational hypothesis.[13] Indeed the importance it has assumed for
him is in itself a testimony to its prevalence in the minds of his
Christian contemporaries. Citing the statements attributed in the
Gospel to Jesus that Elijah had already come and that John the
Baptist 'is the Elijah' whose return had been promised, Tertullian
first questions why we should look to a pagan, Pythagorean
interpretation at all. Then he reminds his readers that the
prophet Elijah did not die as do the majority of men; he was
'translated', carried up in the 'whirlwind to heaven'.[14] So then, he
could not be restored to earth by way of a new body, since he had
never departed from his original body in the first place! No, Elijah
had come back only to fulfil a prophecy. He must have been 'really
and truly the same man, both in respect of his name and his
designation as well as of his unchanged humanity'. That is indeed
a lawyer-like way to read the Bible and I would submit it is
precisely the worst way in which to do so.

Tertullian also raised the customary objection that a reincarnational theory is inconsistent with the increase in the world's
population, which even at that time seemed already alarming.
This objection is still offered by many today; in fact books have
been written on it in comparatively recent years, although now
that we know of the vastness of the galaxies and of the extreme
likelihood that there are millions of inhabited planets besides our
own, the objection has no force today at all. In Tertullian's time,
however, invoking it was more pardonable.

Justin Martyr, an early second-century Christian writer,
discussed transmigration with a Jew named Trypho, but the
outcome of the discussion is not entirely clear. There is no doubt,
however, that before Christian dogmas had been hardened by the
Church, many Christians were taking reincarnational hypotheses
seriously, for (as we have seen earlier) something had to be done
about specifying the Christian hope, now that the imminent
expectation of the *parousia* had waned. Every patristic scholar
knows that the doctrine of the pre-existence of the soul was openly

held by some of the Alexandrian Fathers, including Clement and
Origen, and that is a doctrine which, to say the least, has many
affinities with a reincarnational one of the Pythagorean or
Platonic type. Indeed, many centuries later, Thomas Aquinas,
although he does not hold either a pre-existence or a transmigrationist theory, recognizes, with his usual perspicacity, that
all who have admitted the existence of the soul before birth in a
body admit, at least implicitly, a reincarnationist principle.[15] Nor
was Thomas the first to do so. Christians in the early centuries who
held such doctrines were sometimes called and may have called
themselves the *pre-existiani*.

The Pythagorean and Platonic types of reincarnational theory
were by no means, however, the only ones in the minds of the
Fathers, who were generally also well acquainted with the Stoic
doctrine of palingenesis. According to this doctrine, worlds are
created in infinite succession. As one is destroyed, another comes
into being that is an exact replica of it. Every individual who lived
and died in one world is regenerated in precisely the same way in
the succeeding and in every succeeding world, *ad infinitum*.
Tatian, Clement of Alexandria, and Origen, who were all very
familiar with this influential Stoic doctrine, take note of or at least
hint at an analogy between it and the Christian doctrine of the
resurrection of the body. Predictably, they disapprove of the Stoic
proposal on the ground that it seems to envision no *telos*, no
purpose. It is plain also that a completely cyclic understanding of
history, such as is found in Stoicism, is fundamentally incompatible with the main thrust of Christian belief in free choice and
in a benevolent God who cares for and redeems his creatures.

The fact, however, that despite this obvious incompatibility, the
Fathers perceive any connection at all between this and the
Christian doctrine of resurrection is noteworthy. Both Augustine[16]
and Lactantius[17] go so far as to cite the Stoic theory by way of
arguing, in terms of the philosophical discussions of their day, that
the Christian doctrine of the resurrection is not so foolish as its
adversaries suppose, since it has an analogy in the teachings of that
then very respectable school. Of course no Christian could have
any part in the deterministic presuppositions of the Stoic theory;
nevertheless, a connection was seen. Nemesius mentions the Stoic
theory as something that 'some people' hold.[18] The Fathers note,
generally, that the Stoic doctrine is resurrection to a temporary
life, while the Christian doctrine is resurrection to life everlasting;

but Tatian, at least, detects the fundamental difference: in the Stoic theory there is no useful purpose, no *telos*, while in the Christian doctrine there is, through the judgment. The Stoics had no notion of divine intervention or divine care as Christians understood the ways of God.

Not only was the Stoic philosophy of history, with its strict cyclic determinism, unacceptable to Christian thinkers in that age, as it still must be in our own; it is alien to all that we now know of the evolutionary principle that has so thoroughly affected our scientific understanding of everything in the universe around us. Of course nobody in the ancient world could have perceived the evolutionary principle as today we must. Nevertheless, the fact that Christian thinkers repudiated the Stoic philosophy of history, despite the analogy they thought they saw between Stoic palingenesis and Christian resurrection and despite also the widespread appreciation among Christian thinkers of Stoic ethical ideals, points to their having detected in their own way what was fundamentally wrong with the Stoic theory. It had no room for human development and therefore none for redemption by Christ and resurrection to everlasting life.

Epiphanius, a fourth-century Church Father, reports on the prophecies uttered by the second-century Montanus in the course of which the Holy Spirit is said to have spoken as follows: 'Why do you call a man who has been saved a superman?[19] The notion of moral progress was presupposed by Christians, with its evolutionary implications. This will be more fully dicussed in our later chapter on evolution and the concept of reincarnation in Christian thought. Meanwhile let us simply note that, while the Stoic theory on this subject excluded Christian presuppositions about moral evolution, the transmigrational tradition in Pythagoras and Plato were not merely hospitable on this score; they entailed a thoroughgoing moral evolutionism. That did not by itself make a marriage between Christianity and Platonism inevitable, but it did make it at least feasible and even promising.

In the Pythagorean and Platonic presentations of a reincarnationism the Fathers saw indeed, a closer analogy. We have already noted Tertullian's perception in this matter. Origen quotes Celsus as charging that the Christians had arrived at their resurrection doctrine as a result of having misunderstood the traditional philosophical doctrine of the transmigration of souls.[20] Gregory of Nyssa, as we have already seen, goes so far as to affirm that the traditional theory of the transmigration of souls is not entirely incompatible with the resurrection that is the Christian hope.[21] Other Fathers also note this analogy. Generally speaking, however, they tend to think of the Pythagorean theory in one of its cruder, unethical forms, in which a human soul can be supposed to enter the body of a beast. In contrast to such a theory, they point, of course, to the very different character of the resurrection hope, which is the hope of restoration of one's own body in a glorified form. The misunderstanding is unfortunate, because had the Fathers more adequately understood this type of reincarnationist theory they would have had fewer misgivings about it and would have seen that moral judgment is at the heart of it. What they attack in it is only accidentally found in some crass presentations of the theory and is susceptible to an interpretation much more consonant with the mainstream of the Christian doctrine of God.

Still, the Fathers generally, including Origen, took very seriously the notion that the resurrected body, for all its angelic grandeur, had to be in some way continuous with our present body. Origen held that there is an element common to 'sublunary' bodies, celestial bodies and 'spiritual' bodies such as angels and resurrected human beings. The differences that may exist among them are differences only of degree; for example, in his own words, of *puritas* (purity), *subtilitas* (fineness), and *gloria* (glory).[22] This common element he calls 'aether', which, following Plato,[23] as is Origen's usual inclination, he accounts one of the four elements. (Origen repudiates Aristotle's concept of a fifth element).[24] So he tries to establish a common element providing continuity between our present animal body and the glorified body that is promised us.

Origen then goes on to the question of the meaning of 'the same' body. He notes that our earthly bodies change: I am twice as tall as I was at the age of eight; since my youth my hair has greyed, yet I account myself the same person, having the same body. So the principle of individuation, as Aristotle saw, must be not the stuff but the form, and according to Origen that form is peculiar to me. At the resurrection my soul is to be reunited with that form, which Origen seems to identify with what the Stoics, in a well-known phrase, called the *logos spermatikos*, the 'seminal reason'. So we ought to be careful, according to Origen, not to suppose that 'the same body' means this animal body, with its flesh, bones, lungs, kidneys, and so forth: a body that might be immature (as in children) or crippled or deformed, as have been the bodies of some of the most distinguished members of the human race.

Origen's perspicacity here is acute. To appreciate it fully we should glance at how most of the other early Fathers, by contrast, interpret the question. His language and his thought patterns are not, of course, those that would come naturally to a modern thinker, yet compared with the views of his contemporaries Origen's anticipate what most of us would account an enlightened approach to a subject of this kind. The other Fathers emphasize physical identity. Irenaeus, for instance, in a statement fore-shadowing the pronouncement of the Fourth Lateran Council that I have already quoted in chapter 2, says definitely that those who are resurrected will rise with their very own bodies.[25] Tertullian is even more dogmatic: 'the flesh shall rise again, wholly, in everyman, in its identity, in its absolute integrity'.[26] He even specifies[27] that this includes particular parts of the body such as the teeth, the bowels, and the genitalia. He is not deterred by Jesus's saying that there is to be no marriage in heaven because we are to be as the angels.[28] He points out, following his predilection for literalism, that the Gospels do not say we are to be angels, only that we shall be *like* angels or equal to angels. He even supposes that despite our possession of genitalia we shall have no desire to use them and indeed no use for them,[29] which is surely a most infelicitous vision of organic inefficiency: permanently (indeed everlastingly) functionless yet indispensable appurtenances.

Tertullian, however, is not at a loss to answer such obvious questions. Postulating that all organs must be retrieved and raised up with the resurrection body, he discusses the problem and is forced to conclude that these organs, though no longer having their present function, 'may possibly have something to do'; that is, God will provide them with a function.[30] Others among the early Fathers treat the problem similarly, apparently not seeing that a new function would call for a different instrument and therefore a different body adapted to the new life.[31] What we now know of biological evolution would have made it impossible for these Fathers to engage in such speculations; but had not they been so wedded to a literalistic approach to the Bible they might have avoided conclusions that must have seemed ridiculous even in those times.

Origen, the most learned biblical scholar of his day as well as by far the most creative thinker, succeeded in a remarkable degree both in avoiding such absurdities and constructing a system which, whatever we may think of it, is both coherent and compatible with the apostolic *kerygma*: the promise of new life by resurrection through Jesus Christ. It is largely to exhibit his stature and importance that I have dwelt on the literalism of some of the other Fathers and its consequences. Origen's views, we shall see, became eventually unfashionable in the Church and in the minds of many were tainted with heresy, while a cruder literalism prospered. What precisely he taught on the subject of reincarnation is, for reasons to be presently given, not entirely clear, although I can see little cause to doubt that he held this doctrine in one form or another, and he certainly taught the pre-existence of the soul.

Origen is by any reckoning an extraordinary figure. Born in Egypt, probably at Alexandria, about the year AD 185, he received at home a thoroughly Christian education. He is generally believed to have been the pupil of Clement of Alexandria, although some scholars have questioned this.[32] During the persecution of Christians in the year 202, Origen's father was killed. So passionate and impetuous was the youthful Origen that his mother had to hide his clothes to prevent his going forth to invite martyrdom for himself. At an astonishingly early age that attests the precocity of his genius, he was chosen to succeed Clement as head of the Alexandrian school. Hardly less remarkable than his intellectual prowess was his personal Christian commitment and self-discipline. Everyone knows of the excess of zeal that caused him to castrate himself, in obedience to what he took at the time to be a Gospel injunction[33] and perhaps also because he supposed that the deprivation, by removing sexual exigencies, would enable him both to think with greater detachment and to serve God and the Church more diligently. We must see that notorious episode in the context of the age in which he lived and the peculiar circumstances of his life. At any rate, he matured into an intellectual giant and gave his life to the scholarly service of the Church. Eventually, in the persecution under Decius in the year 250, he was imprisoned and severely tortured. He died a few years later.

Such was Origen's desire to serve the students who worked under him that he sought to broaden his influence by going to study pagan philosophy under Ammonias Saccas, regarded as the founder of the Neoplatonic school. The importance Neoplatonism was to assume in the Gentile world would be difficult to exaggerate. It is not too much to say that it became a formidable rival that might well have triumphed over Christianity in the long run but for its being too intellectual for the masses. Christian thinkers, notably Augustine in the West, saw their Christian faith through its eyes. So Origen, sitting at the feet of its reputed founder, was meeting what was to be the major intellectual challenge of the pagan world. He could not but have been deeply aware of the transmigrational view. He travelled to Rome and to Palestine, where he preached at the invitation of the Bishops of Caesarea and Aelia, whereupon he was disciplined by his own bishop, Demetrius, on the ground that he had preached without being ordained priest. For about twelve years he devoted himself almost exclusively to literary work. Again he visited Palestine, this time in 230, when he was ordained priest by the bishops who had invited him, whereupon, for an alleged irregularity in his ordination, Demetrius then deprived him of his teaching position, deposed him from the priesthood, and exiled him: a triple action that we must surely attribute to petty ecclesiastical spite. Origen found refuge at Caesarea, where he went on with his literary work and established a school that acquired much fame. He preached faithfully till his last trials.

Origen's most important philosophical work, *Peri archōn* (*De principiis*), is a systematic exposition of Christian teaching in four books, which treat respectively of (1) God and the angels, (2) man and the material world, (3) free will and its consequences, and (4) the Bible. Origen takes as his point of departure on all subjects, belief in the unity of God. He develops an elaborate and highly original theory of creation and salvation. Creation is eternal, for God must be always active. All spirits are created equal, but through the exercise of their free will some sinned and so became either demons or else humans imprisoned in carnal bodies. Death is not the end for humans; they may turn into demons or angels and may so go on making progress or regress, always according to the exercise of their free will, through a succession of long ages or aeons. The process takes an enormously long time, an incalculably long series of such aeons. What he teaches about salvation is very much like the typical Indian doctrine of karma, along with the Christian doctrine of Providence. According to Origen, each soul is embodied once in each aeon. He *seems* to reject those forms of reincarnationism that teach multiple embodiments in one single aeon.[34] Then at the final apocatastasis, all creatures, including the Devil himself, will be saved. So while of course he rejects certain forms of reincarnationist theory, as we have seen, he constructs an impressive system that cannot be made intelligible without some form of reincarnationism. He insists, however, on purpose and growth: no teaching that does not provide for these essential aspects of the Christian hope is acceptable to him.

As we might expect in a man of such calibre, he was a controversial figure in his own day and was long to remain so. He gained much popularity and encountered much opposition. Never had the Church a more devoted son. He sought to ground all his teaching in Holy Scripture. He was by no means alone among the Fathers in his use of the Platonic tradition. No thinking person of his time could have avoided so influential a force. No doubt he was especially influenced by a fundamental concept of that tradition: the soul is superior to the body that imprisons it and that yet is its instrument. The body restricts the soul as the marble restricts the sculptor who nevertheless can do nothing without it. A view of this sort is at any rate conducive to reincarnationism. If Origen did reject transmigration (which I think not to be the case) then it must have been for some biblical reason that he found compelling. In view of the elaborate philosophical and theological system he was able to construct, it is not easy to see that he could have found anything in Scripture that would have compelled such a resolute Christian Platonist to rule out the transmigration of the soul.

What, then, does the text say? Alas, in the case of Origen, that is not the straightforward question that it looks and that it ought to be. For his friends imposed a sort of informal censorship on passages in his works that they thought might cast a shadow over his orthodoxy. Many passages and some works that probably contained his most interesting speculations were allowed, therefore, to disappear. What remains survives only in fragments or in free Latin translations. Origen was one of the most prolific writers in all Christian literature. The length of some of his works no doubt provided his friends with a pretext for abbreviating them by expurgating the most intellectually adventuresome sections. Disapproving scribes simply let them vanish. Most of his commentaries on books of the Bible survive only in small fragments. Of the *De principiis* we have now only a free Latin translation of the original Greek text. The work of Tyrannius Rufinus (*c.* 345-410), it is far from what one would like to have. There can be no doubt that Rufinus bowdlerized Origen in the interests of protecting him from his adversaries who sought to prove him a heretic. Jerome, celebrated for his translation of the Bible into Latin, was a contemporary of Rufinus and noted the tendentious character of Rufinus's translations.

The result of this unfortunate situation is that it is virtually impossible to find a text that proves that Origen upheld a doctrine of the transmigration of the soul without being confronted with another that seems to show plainly that he rejected such a doctrine. He writes, for example, of 'the false doctrine of the transmigration of souls into bodies'.[35] This may well refer, however, to a particular *kind* of transmigrational theory. Of course Origen would repudiate some forms of it, much as the Church of England's Articles of Religion condemned 'the Romish Doctrine concerning Purgatory' without thereby by any means ruling out all doctrines of the intermediate state, such as the Tractarians were to develop centuries later. Origen certainly rejected, for instance, the Stoic doctrine to which allusion has already been made, since the cyclic theory of history inseparable from it would have been antithetical to both the testimony of the Bible and his own philosophical system.

We do find, however, some clear witness to what Origen held on pre-existence and, at least by implication, on the transmigration of souls. For example:

> All rational creatures who are incorporeal and invisible, if they become negligent, gradually sink to a lower level and take to themselves bodies suitable to the regions into which they descend; that is to say, first, ethereal bodies, and then aereal. And when they reach the neighourhood of the earth they are enclosed in grosser bodies, and last of all are tied to human flesh. It is a mark of extreme negligence and sloth for any soul to descend and lose its own nature so completely as to be bound, in consequence of its vices, to the gross body of one of the irrational animals.[36].

Again:

> When the soul falls away from the good and inclines towards evil it becomes more and more involved in this process of degradation. Then, unless it turns back, it is rendered brutish by its folly and bestial by its wickedness and it is carried towards the condi-

tions of unreason and, so to speak, of the watery life. Then, as befits the degree of its fall into evil, it is clothed with the body of this or that irrational animal.[37]

Jerome, seeking to show his readers that Origen did believe in the transmigration of the soul, charges him with having made the following statement, which he cites and which is omitted in Rufinus's translation:[38]

If anyone can show that incorporeal and rational nature, when deprived of a body, can live by itself, and that it is in a worse condition when clothed with a body and in a better when it lays the body aside, then no one can doubt that bodies did not exist in the beginning, but are now created at intervals on account of the different movements of rational creatures, in order to supply a covering to such as need it; and that on the other hand, when these creatures have risen out of the degradation of their falls to a better condition, the bodies are dissolved into nothing; and that these changes go on happening for ever.

In the Greek text of Origen we also read:

It must needs be that the nature of bodies is not primary, but that it was created at intervals on account of certain falls that happened to rational beings who came to need bodies; and again, that when their restoration is perfectly accomplished these bodies are dissolved into nothing, so that this is for ever happening.[39]

According to Jerome, Origen teaches that 'after many aeons and the one restoration of all things, the state of Gabriel will be the same as that of the Devil, Paul's as that of Caiaphas, that of virgins as that of prostitutes'.[40] This passage not only exhibits Origen's well-known universalism; it also strongly suggests a reincarnational schema. The lengthy and complex process that is envisioned seems, especially in light of what else is known of Origen's views, to imply a schema of that kind.

Origen's thoroughly biblical orientation kept him securely within the orbit of Christian orthodoxy. By no means can he be accounted fundamentally deviant or heretical, for although he uses his clear mind and his great learning very freely in the service of the Christian faith he keeps all focused on the documents of the Christian heritage: the Bible.

Origenism was a very different matter. In the late fourth century it became the focus of an acrimonious controversy, too complex for the needs or scope of the present chapter. Ecclesiastico-political motives played, as so often in the history of the Church, a very large part in the controversies. The ambitious patriarch of Alexandria, Theophilus, eventually invoked a council at Alexandria that condemned Origenism in the year 400. Theophilus called Origen the 'hydra of heresies'. In the sixth century the controversy was renewed in a somewhat different form. By this time the name of Origen was used by many as a cloak for promoting various pantheistic movements, much as the names of Calvin and of Freud have been used for promoting opinions that they would not have condoned. The Origenistic controversy was embedded, moreover, in a larger framework of controversy over other issues that were by this time troubling the Church. The disputes about Origenism were part of a much larger dispute that eventually led to the disastrous schism between East and West in 1054.

So complex and extensive were the political moves within which the Origenist controversy was pursued in the sixth century that it is extremely difficult to assess what it really was apart from them. Origenist monks were divided into two main groups: the Isochrists and the Protoctists. According to the former, all human beings are destined to become eventually equal to Christ, which was of course a heretical notion. The Protoctists denied that tenet. They ended by repudiating the doctrine of the pre-existence of the soul. At length the Emperor Justinian called an ecumenical council: the Second Council of Constantinople, known also as the Fifth Ecumenical Council of the Christian Church. It met in 553. Its purpose was the comprehensive one of trying to reconcile differences between East and West. Justinian hoped also to conciliate the Monophysites, who taught that Christ had only one nature, the divine, by attacking their opponents, the Nestorians. Monophysitism was a widespread view. Despite the affirmation at the Council of Chalcedon in 451 that Christ had two natures, the divine and the human, the tendency to exalt the divine at the expense of the human was considerable and in popular piety in the later Middle Ages it was to become very marked. Justinian, in his edict of 543-544, had condemned certain writings sympathetic to

Nestorius, in what came to be called *ta tria kephalaia*, 'The Three Chapters'. Much that the Council was called to accomplish and did discuss had nothing at all to do with Origen and most of Justinian's clumsy efforts were in any case unproductive. It is very difficult to tell, indeed, whether Origen was condemned at all.

Of the fourteen anathemas pronounced by the Council, Origen's name is mentioned in one, among a list of heretics, and it is unclear whether that mention was in fact original or a later interpolation. Not only was the outcome of the Council inconclusive: one cannot always be sure precisely what the inconclusiveness was about. What does seem fairly clear is that Origen's name was used as that of a convenient whipping-boy, often with little or no understanding of the subtleties of his thought. In an atmosphere of such political conniving and bitter hostility about so many things, anything resembling a fair consideration of so difficult a question as that of the trans-migration of the soul within the context of the Christian hope was plainly impossible.

We all know how far removed a movement can stray from the thought of the man after whom it takes its name. As I have already hinted, Calvin would have been outraged by what some of the later Calvinists attributed to him and Freud astonished by what is often said in his name. So with Origen; in one way or another he got a bad press. His name came to be associated with heretical movements, although as in all such smear tactics nobody saw very clearly or could have seen what exactly were the heresies attributed to him. What the Fifth Ecumenical Council attacked was Origenism, not Origen. One result, however, was that the doctrine of the pre-existence of the soul, and then by implication that of transmigration in any form, was simply excluded from further consideration by those who sought to show themselves orthodox.

The West was never very skilful in understanding the subtleties of Greek thought, and Origen's thought was very Greek indeed. What G. L. Prestige once said of the triumph of Chalcedon applies even more strikingly to later controversies in which East and West were engaged: 'the clumsy occident intervened as teacher in a matter which it had not properly learned and did not really understand.'[41] But when to the political machinations of Byzantium were added both the theological incomprehension of the Latin-speaking West and the well-meaning bowdlerizing of Origen's own friends, any genuine understanding of anything that he had taught on so delicate and intricate a question as the nature of the soul's pilgrimage could not be but effectively distorted if not destroyed.

What we find above all in Christian literature in the first few centuries, including the New Testament itself, is that among the thinkers and intellectual leaders of the Christian Way the concept of the transmigration of the soul did not in itself call for either endorsement or renunciation, although some attacked certain forms of it that they knew. Such attacks show us how widespread the concept must have been within the Christian fold, for there is never any point in attacking teachings that command no interest among your audience. As we have seen, transmigrationism was in the air in the Mediterranean world in which Christianity was cradled, but because of the imminent expectation of the end of the present age by the first generation or two of the followers of the Way, speculation about it seemed pointless. As that hope receded and Christian missionaries had to meet the Gentile world on its own ground and according to its own patterns of thought, that situation changed. While certain forms of transmigrationism seemed alien, by no means all had to be so regarded. The immense respect for Plato among the Fathers naturally engendered interest in the reincarnationist tradition he had inherited from revered ways of thought in the repositories of ancient wisdom.

The confused state of Christian eschatology could not but have stimulated, as we have seen it did, an interest in the concept of reincarnation. Why, then, was it frowned upon at all? Who had reason to oppose it? Why did a concept so intellectually promising in terms of the thought of the latter days of the ancient world and the dawn of the new one we call the Middle Ages have to go underground, as indubitably it did? Without prejudging the merits or demerits of the reincarnationist concept within the Christian framework of ideas, we must ask why it should have been so threatening to the power-structures of the day as to be so much feared and opposed?. Wherein lay the threat of such a seemingly innocuous idea? To such questions as these we must turn in our next chapter.

5 How and Why Reincarnationism Fell Into Disfavour

Yet each man kills the thing he loves.

Oscar Wilde, *Ballad of Reading Gaol*

If some form or forms of reincarnationism could seem so worthy of consideration in the eyes of even some Christians in early times, for which we have seen some evidence, why did the notion fade so completely from the centre of the Christian scene? The question, inevitable by any reckoning, becomes perhaps even more pressing when we find, as we do, how conspicuous is the role it has played in Judaism during the Christian era. For Christianity, unlike Hinduism and Buddhism, has a common ancestry with Judaism, so that if reincarnationism in any form were fundamentally alien to Christianity, one might reasonably expect it to be also alien to Judaism, as would certainly be, for instance, a denial of the unity of God or of his righteousness or fatherly care. We find, however, the opposite: while both Judaism and Christianity have remained faithful, each in its own way, to these basic biblical teachings, reincarnation has prospered in Jewish thought. Josephus and Philo in the first century both seem to approve it;[1] in the kabbalistic tradition, which has very ancient roots and flourished in the Middle Ages, it is a fundamental belief; and in hasidic Judaism, which has kabbalistic connections, it is an almost universal belief, expressed throughout that highly influential movement, for instance, in Yiddish literature, in the *Dybbuk* and in the writings of Sholem Asch. Is there then some element peculiar to Christian thought that absolutely excludes it? If not, why has it been lost to the mainstream of Christian tradition?

In very early Christian times, when the speedy end of the age was expected, there might have been some reason to set trans-

60

migrationist views aside. When that hope faded and thinkers
began to see the need for an intermediate state, such objections
could not have retained whatever weight they might have had in
the first century, for as we shall see in our next chapter, a
reincarnationist doctrine of some kind could have functioned very
well indeed in terms of such a cleansing or purgative process. The
objection that because reincarnationism probably came most
commonly in a platonic form it would have seemed to deny the
biblical view of man could not have been by any means a decisive
one, for most of the Fathers were Platonists or else at least much
affected by Platonic modes of thought. Nor would other objections
such as might occur to some churchmen today arise in the minds of
the Fathers; they did not think like us. All this is not to say that we
ought to expect a form of reincarnationism to have been placed at
the centre of Christian tradition, as were eventually doctrines such
as the Incarnation, the Resurrection, and Prevenient Grace. What
we might nevertheless expect is that, if we look only at the
implications of Christian faith as it emerged and was developed in
the experience of those who followed the Christian Way, some
form of reincarnationism should have survived within Christian
thought as a lively if controversial option in the same way as, for
example, the view for Roman Catholics till 1854 that Mary was
conceived without original sin. In terms of medieval and later
Catholic thought there were indeed cogent arguments on both
sides of that question. Yet we find no such situation with respect to
the transmigrationist tradition, although there is nothing in the
development of Christian experience or thought that need have
prevented its having retained at least a similarly optional status
and controversial role.

Is there anything in the concept of reincarnation itself that
might provoke hostility on the part of the hierarchy of the Church?
At first sight it may seem that, so long as we assume that there were
no basic theological objections to the concept, there could be no
reason why it should engender ecclesiastical opposition any more
than any other doctrine such as, say, redemption or grace, sin or
forgiveness. A little reflection, however, will soon help us to see
why it could provoke antagonism on the part of ecclesiastical
leaders. For in contrast to most of the salient elements in Christian
theological systems, it has a special tendency to cause those who
believe in it to feel able to dispense with the institutional aspects of
the Christian Way. That is not to say that they would necessarily

wish to dispense with them; it does mean, however, that they would tend to become aware of being able to fend for themselves spiritually, *if need be*. For reincarnational systems of belief particularly call attention to the role of the individual will. They stress freedom of choice and the individual's capacity to make or mar his or her own destiny. My destiny is up to me. The Church may be immensely helpful to me. I may deeply reverence its teachings and thirst for its sacraments. I may passionately love the life of the Church. Yet if I accept a reincarnationist view I recognize that *in the last resort* I can do without the Church, as a boy can do without his mother, deeply though he may love her. Few Church leaders are either humble enough or sufficiently mature in the spiritual life to be ready so to abdicate power. Of course other doctrines may be so interpreted as to cause spiritual maturation. No thoughtful and educated person, however, can take any developed form of reincarnationism seriously without being confronted with the vision of individual responsibility that makes that kind of growing up inevitable.

We turn, therefore, to political, institutional forces for an explanation. While the Christian communities scattered throughout the Mediterranean in apostolic times had, of course, an organization of some sort, and while 'false doctrine' was a concern of Paul and others in that age, organisation was comparatively loose and attitude to doctrine comparatively open. Once again, expectation of the Second Coming discouraged long-range plans for elaborate ecclesiastical structure and made rigid theological definition seem beside the point. Even after that expectation faded, Christians seem to have been on the whole in no hurry to tighten either doctrine or organisation. By about the middle of the second century, however, a movement in those directions set in.

The causes were complex, but Gnostic influence was, to say the least, one of the most important. Scholars today recognize more than ever before, as a result of discoveries such as the Qumran scrolls and the Nag Hammadi library, that Gnosticism was a far more powerful force in the background of Christianity than scholars formerly supposed. By no means all would agree with Jung's assertion that 'the central ideas of Christianity are rooted in Gnostic philosophy';[2] nevertheless, the importance of Gnosticism for an understanding of Christian beginnings is now much recognized by biblical scholars.[3] No longer can anyone suppose, as was customary fifty years ago, that the Gnostic movement that troubled the Church in the second century can be dismissed as a mere ideological oddity, the creation of wild and fuzzy-minded deviants. That some, perhaps many, of the Gnostic sects whose names have survived, such as the Valentinians, used Gnostic notions in weird ways is not to be denied; but it has been the fate of all religious movements to be ill represented by some of their votaries. We must ask, rather, what was the nature of the Gnostic movement and what precipitated the Church's hardening against it?

This is an exceptionally difficult question, for Gnosticism, as we have seen, was not a philosophical school such as were the Stoics and certainly not a church. There were no Gnostic temples. It was, rather, a climate of thought: an extremely pervasive one. It encouraged turning to ancient sources of wisdom and going beyond the symbols of popular religion to truths Gnostic teachers said were to be found underlying them. Transmigrationism in various forms found ready hospitality in such a climate. Without embarking on the very controversial issues relating to the nature of those particular sects that flourished so vigorously in the second century, waving the Christian banner yet saturated with Gnostic attitudes and probably exaggerating and distorting the wisdom that had been imbibed from Gnostic sources, let us simply say that for one reason or another the Church's leaders were alarmed by the spread of these sects and their influence on the minds of the faithful. No doubt that influence seemed to them to bode ill for the survival of the Church, which must have looked in danger of being dissipated into the haze of doctrinal vacuity they saw encircling it. Leaders such as Irenaeus, for instance, apparently felt the need to make a stand against the inroads of this inchoate yet powerful influence.

So we see the beginnings of new emphases in the Church, notably the institutional emphasis. The faithful are urged to listen to the bishop as the focus of the apostolic tradition and the custodian of the faith. Alongside of this tendency we find a struggle to exclude some doctrines and approve others. As part of these general developments we find, about the end of that century, the fixing of the New Testament canon, that is, the selection out of a prolific early Christian literature of a certain number of books corresponding approximately to the New Testament as we know it today, which were accounted 'regular' and safe from heresies. The heresies from which they were accounted safe were to a

considerable extent, if not predominantly, Gnostic in character.
The motivation of the Church leaders who engaged in this struggle to save the identity of the Church from what they took to be extraneous and unwanted influences is plainly not determinable with any precision, but we all know how jealously the leaders of any organisation hold on to such power and authority as is conceded to them either by tradition or by acclamation. This has always been notably the case in the Church and has come to be widely recognized as one of the Church's greatest weaknesses as a conduit of spirituality. Hence, in later ages, the movements away from the hierarchy to freer societies within the Church, such as those of the medieval friars, which in turn became as they prospered, hidebound in their own way. So we can confidently say that such fears were not absent from the minds of the Church leaders of the second century, who felt so urgently the need to rigidify the constitutional documents of the Church (the New Testament canon), the approved teaching of the Church, and not least its institutional aspect, so that they could control the organisation. All this is very human, very natural, but the result was, of course, the arbitrary exclusion of ideas that might have been of immense value in the development of Christian thought. Paradoxically, the New Testament canon itself is saturated with Gnostic ideas, expressed discreetly rather than blatantly.

In Alexandria, scholars like Clement and Origen pursued their work, as scholars will, in comparative independence of the political turmoils of the Church. We have seen, however, something of the persecution Origen suffered. The Alexandrian Fathers were working within the Church; why, then, the enmity they evoked? As we have seen, the situation by the sixth century had become so confused that it is difficult to tell whether or not it would be accurate to say that reincarnationist teachings were specifically and formally condemned. In any case, that is of little consequence since the practical result was that the Church, in which structure, organisation, and dogmatic formulation had by then clearly hardened, successfully caused these teachings to disappear from public view and be forced underground. Why did the suppression of a religious idea that seems, whether we like it or not, at least both reasonable and innocuous, come to be treated with such hostility?

We shall find much of the answer as we look at the re-emergence of the idea in the twelfth century when the Albigenses, who espoused it, suffered persecution tantamount to genocide. They had a long ancestry. Similar groups had arisen earlier, but not in quite the same political circumstances. In the fifth century, in Syria, the Gnostic Paulicians, who included reincarnationism in their teachings, had grown rapidly. In the tenth century we encounter the Bogomils in Bulgaria, who seem to have had a Paulician ancestry. In 1118 the leader of the movement, which had spread to Constantinople, was burnt by order of the Emperor. A synod ordered the destruction of their books in 1140. Groups of a similar sort spread along the commercial routes into central Europe, known by various names and often called Cathari or 'pure ones'. Their theology was dualistic, their mode of life ascetic.

The most famous of these groups appeared early in the eleventh century in the south of France. They became known as the Albigenses, from the city of Albi. They were anti-Church, anti-sacramental, vegetarian, and reincarnationist. Their ethical teachings remind the modern reader of those of the Quakers in seventeenth-century England: harmlessness, pacifism, chastity, reverence for all living beings and strictness in truth-telling. The common people saw in them a contrast to the lives of the clergy, which in that time and place were at a low moral ebb. Their success was immense, so much so that some historians have suggested that by the end of the twelfth century they had so captivated the south of France and the north of Italy as to challenge the very institutional survival of the Church.

The teachings of the Albigenses were condemned by various Church councils: one at Reims in 1148, one at Verona in 1184, and the Fourth Lateran Council in 1215, to which we have already referred and at which certain Church doctrines were defined with particular reference to the teachings of the Albigensian heretics. Pope Innocent III sent out missionaries to convert them: first the Cistercians, then the Dominicans. These missions were conspicuously unsuccessful. The Pope then organized a crusade calculated to persuade the heretics by more militaristic methods. Battles were waged against the Albigenses, often involving cruel massacres. These campaigns culminated in the Battle of Muret in 1213, in which Simon de Montfort decisively defeated the leader of the Albigenses, Peter of Aragon. Finally, in 1233 Pope Gregory IX charged the Dominican Order of Preachers, through the Inquisition, with the task of exterminating any surviving representatives of the movement. By the end of the fourteenth century we hear no more of them.

That the Church's extreme fear of the Albigensian movement
was not entirely based on theological disapproval of some of their
more extravagantly ascetic modes of thought and life, such as total
sexual abstinence among the *perfecti*,[4] can be shown by the fact
that when the Church tightened the discipline of its own clergy it
did so along the lines of the Albigensian ideals. The Church
hierarchy's fear was due, rather, to the threat they saw in the power
structure of the ecclesiastical institution. For the Albigenses
removed from the minds of the people the sense of dependence on
ecclesiastical machinery. The fear of hell, for example, was
removed, and they also preached against purgatory in the penal
form in which it was being presented by the medieval Latin
Church.

No doubt the anti-institutional elements in Albigensian
teaching naturally antagonized the clergy. At the centre of
Albigensian belief, however, was the ancient doctrine of the
transmigration of souls. This, more than anything else in their
teaching, was the mainspring of the independence of ecclesiastical
control that they were able to inculcate into their followers. For as I
have already suggested, although one may be a believer in
reincarnation and at the same time a reverent and faithful
member of the Church, one is at least on the way to being able to
dispense with the external control of one's life by the Church and
also to minimise the importance of ritual, however helpful its
niceties may be as an aid to one's pilgrimage. Reincarnationist
belief in its developed, ethical form so focuses moral and spiritual
progress on the individual and so invests him or her with
responsibility for personal salvation, that the Church, useful and
commendable instrument though it may be in its way, can no
longer have the indispensable role that its institutional leaders
naturally prefer it to play.

It is therefore not difficult to see that in the circumstances of the
medieval Church the reincarnationist teachings of the Albigenses
would look almost as intolerable to the Church's hierarchy as
would a pacifist oration in an army officers' mess. Belonging to the
Church relieved one of a large part of the burden of personal
responsibility for salvation. The Church could be generous, not to
say indulgent, to those who followed the rules, assuring them of a
relatively easy passage through this life, through purgatory, and
into heaven. The price was, however, total reliance on the Church
as the indispensable instrument of God. Once the paternalism of

the Church was challenged, as it was by a doctrine such as reincarnation, people would become less dependent children and more independent adults in their pilgrimage towards salvation, and the medieval Church was not adaptable to such a state of affairs. It would have fatally injured priestly power.

With the Neoplatonic revival that began in Florence in the fifteenth century, which Italians call the Quattrocento, came renewed interest in reincarnationism. The Quattrocento Renaissance, under the powerful patronage of the Medici, could not but encourage an individualistic approach to all human activity. Renaissance man, ever seeking to go back to the original sources, found in Plato and Plotinus many ideas that had been distorted or obscured in the course of the intervening centuries, and among them, of course, was that of the transmigration of souls. Pico della Mirandola, in his celebrated *Oration on the Dignity of Man,* specifically taught that the soul passes out of one body and enters another one. Georgius Gemistus Plethon, a native of Constantinople, who was much admired by Cosmo de' Medici, had Cardinal Bessarion among his disciples and wrote a defence of the Eastern Church's doctrine of the Procession of the Holy Spirit, openly argued for transmigrationism,

The Renaissance did bring in its train, as we shall see later, a climate of thought in which transmigrationism could be seriously discussed and by many eagerly accepted. That was largely because the *umanisti*, besides being so deeply affected by Platonic modes of thought, were individualists and fostered an individualist type of outlook. The Church itself was deeply influenced by the new individualism. It affected, for instance, the Society of Jesus, that great institution of Ignatius of Loyola: a strange mixture of chivalric medieval militarism and humanistic Renaissance individualism. The Reformation Fathers were likewise indebted to the Renaissance, without which they could not have gone as they did to the biblical sources of the Christian faith. The Reformation *was* a biblical renaissance. Luther and Calvin, though thoroughly medieval in the general mould of their thought, could not be untouched by the spirit of their age. Yet when all that is said, we must recognize that forces in the Church, on both sides of the Reformation curtain, felt reason to fear reincarnationist concepts and sought to belittle and, where possible, oust them.

The reason for this fear, which is by no means moribund even in our own day, is much the same as it was in much earlier times. The

concept of reincarnation is associated with an individualistic programme in which one can be, in an emergency, so to speak, able to
dispense with the ministrations of the Church. I repeat that by no
means does this mean or ever did mean that one necessarily wishes
to do so. On the contrary, doing so may be peculiarly painful. Yet
one is no longer absolutely dependent on the Church, Roman or
Orthodox, Anglican or Reformed, for one's passage through this
life to one's salvation and eventual goal. Such spiritual independence could never, of course, disturb thoughtful bishops and others
who, being themselves advanced in the pilgrimage, could not but
welcome the attainments of others. Least of all could they be
frightened by the spiritual independence of the few, when they
have to cope with the dependence of so many. Those in the
hierarchy (unfortunately numerous) who are far behind even those
whom they purport to lead, are, however, very much threatened
indeed by such manifestations of independent spiritual capacity.

All this is regrettable, of course, because the more advanced one
is in the spiritual pilgrimage the more aware one is of the need for
help from others more advanced still. The saints have grasped at
any straw they could find in the Church from which they might
hope to find help. One may always learn something, even from the
least advanced, but generally speaking the saints have had to rely
more and more on invisible helpers, of whom something will be
said in a later chapter. The role of such helpers is an important
part of the Church's tradition.

Be all that as it may, all the evidence points to the fact that the
ancient doctrine of transmigrationism has been consciously and
unconsciously feared by the Church's hierarchies for no other
reason than that it is particularly and in a peculiar way associated
with spiritual independence. Independence from the Church is the
last thing that I or any other Christian would seek to encourage;
but the capacity for it is invaluable. When, for one reason or
another, soldiers are separated from their unit, the battle, and
indeed the course of the war, can often depend on their ability to
function on their own. This is by no means less true of the soldiers
of Christ.

6 Reincarnation as an Interpretation of Purgatory

The training that men call punishments.

Clement of Alexandria, *Stromateis*

We have seen that from early times some Christian thinkers found pre-existence and rebirth to be concepts at least worthy of serious consideration and that a tradition prospered within Christian thought that was hospitable to such an element in human history and destiny. We have seen, too, some of the reasons why such a tradition was forced underground and how, despite persecution and the terrors of the Inquisition, it kept re-appearing within the Christian fold, being a concept favoured by some of the most eminent luminaries of Western thought and of its most creative writers. It seems plausible to some, perhaps even incontestable, that it is at least not *fundamentally* incompatible with a Christian view of our pilgrimage. How, then, precisely might we propose to fit it into a Christian vision of our destiny and hail it as an aspect of our Christian hope?

I propose that we start by looking at the ancient doctrine of the intermediate state in terms of a series of rebirths on this and other planets. The proposal has the merit of being more intelligible than most accounts of purgatory, even the more enlightened ones. It fits peculiarly well into the understanding of the intermediate state as developed in Anglican thought, for instance, under Tractarian influence, as one of development and growth. Such a concept does not exclude, of course, the prospect of discipline and pain as elements in the training that growth and development entail. Reincarnationist doctrines are quite startlingly apposite. Reincarnation, functioning as the intermediate state, while it would not express itself in the penal terms traditional in Roman Catholic theology on the subject of purgatory, would not be alien to anything accounted essential in that theological tradition. It

69

would be, moreover, peculiarly susceptible, at least in some important respects, to being treated as parallel to certain visions of purgatory described by the saints, of which the most notable is that of Catherine of Genoa, a fifteenth-century married noble-woman of extraordinary spiritual sensitivity and perception.

Describing the moment of death and entry into purgatory, she says that only at that moment does the soul know precisely what is the cause of its need for its purgatorial destination. Never again will it have this acute awareness, which, through self-concern, would impede its progress. At this crucial moment, however, the soul, seeing the nature of the imperfection that impedes it from attaining its end, which is God, and that there is no way the impediment can be removed except by purgatory, 'swiftly and of its own accord (*volontieri*) casts itself into it.'[1] The notion of the soul's sharp awareness of its need and of its plunging itself into purgatory, where it may no longer remember precisely why it is there, is a breathtaking parallel to what reincarnationists typically say about the choice of a new womb for rebirth. This is not, of course, to say that anything of this sort was in Catherine's mind. The parallel is, however, so astonishing as to suggest that the one is simply a mythological translation of the truth the other contains.

Then, as she goes on to describe the condition of the soul in purgatory, she asserts that it is no longer capable of any such choice. It has to carry on.[2] This aspect of Catherine's vision also fits: the average person has no answer to existentialist questions such as 'why am I here?' unless by invoking a theological belief. Many people would account such a question silly or futile, like asking a physicist why the universe is there or a Christian why God is there in the first place. They simply find themselves here and can attribute the circumstance only to their parents' reproductive activities. They think we all are, as the nihilist Sartre poignantly puts it in a well-known phrase, *jeté là, comme ça.* According to the reincarnationist, there is an excellent, indeed the perfect, reason for my being here in precisely the circumstances in which I find myself: I *chose* it, seeing it to be right for me. Now I am too busy working at my task to remember precisely why I embraced it. This is exactly what Catherine says about the state of the soul in purgatory, after that moment of intense self-awareness in which it has plunged itself thither.

So while the next step on our way is to be seen as purgatorial, we have been 'in purgatory' for many lifetimes already and are in the midst of one now. This schema accords well with the modern existentialist language that speaks of circumstance, that which stands around and hems us in, as our challenge in life. We are like prisoners-of-war whose prime duty is to escape; yet there are no easy ways, no short cuts. The prison that is human life is, however, in one important respect different from any prisoner-of-war camp. We have chosen it ourselves, each one of us for his or her own training. We have given ourselves, each one of us, a puzzle to solve. It is a hard and painful process, more so for some than for others, yet no life is without its trials, its disappointments, its woes. The fact that I have chosen mine does not in the least diminish the trials that attend it. The young man whose supreme longing was to get into the Commandos or the Marines does not on that account find life thereafter plain sailing.

Human life, however, is not all hardship and trial. In even the most troubled and tragic lives there is joy. While suffering is the inevitable concomitant of any genuine development and of any authentic growth, so also is at least some measure of fulfilment and joy. Life is indeed on the whole more a struggle than a hymn, yet beyond the noise of battle we do at least sometimes catch the descant of the angels' song. Here again is a parallel between the reincarnationist's account of the situation and what is traditionally said about purgatory. Purgatory, for all the pain inseparable from the cleansing process, is also described as a state of joy because (unlike the hopelessness of hell) it carries with it the awareness that one is on one's way to God, which is what the Christian finds characteristic of his or her earthly pilgrimage. It is not a penal sentence; it is, rather, a spiritual reformatory. Through all the grinding tasks runs at least a strain of joy, an assurance of purpose. For Christians, 'all things work together for good for those who love God and are called according to his purpose.'[3]

Fire is the traditional symbol of purification. All is 'tried by fire'. The pains of purgatory, traditionally, are fiery. According to the ancient Orphic myth, cremation of the body was believed to assist in the purification of the soul. Where the Christian Fathers entertain a concept of the intermediate state, the purificatory process is generally conceived as fiery, as in Clement of Alexandria, who specifically alludes to purifying fire.[4] Origen develops the same concept, for which those who have adopted any concept of the intermediate state have generally found their biblical support in an allusion of Paul's to the notion that some are saved 'yet so as by fire'.[5] Destruction of the whole world by fire was a characteristic theme of Palestinian Jewish literature, of which we have an echo in the New Testament prediction that the heavens, being on fire, shall be dissolved, and the elements shall melt with extreme heat.[6] In Catherine's imagery, the purgatorial fire consumes all the dross but cannot consume the gold, which is impervious to it. That is to say, the soul, when completely purified, cannot suffer any more; it no longer feels the fire. The gold has been in the fire all along, for the fire is God, but while the gold was mixed with the dross the soul suffered pain; now that the dross is gone so has the pain. Nothing is left but joy.

Once again the reincarnationist parallel suggests itself. The sufferings we endure in life may look as though brought on by an external force, but they are really brought upon ourselves. As soon as we are cured of the disease that makes us sensitive to the pain (a self-induced disease), we feel the pain no more. The medicine tastes abominable, nauseating me; but as soon as its work is done I experience a sense of well-being where only yesterday I was tormented by fiery pains.

On the reincarnationist view, one little life of whatever length (a few days or a hundred years) is not enough to weed out the garden of the soul. Weeds keep coming up, time after time, choking the good seed. The purificatory process takes a far longer time than we are likely to imagine. As we once thought of the whole history of the evolution of mankind in terms of a few thousand years and must now think in millions of years, so we must develop a wider spectrum in thinking about human salvation.

Yet those who adhered to the traditional purgatorial concept perceived this in their own way, for the classic theologians who treat it extensively assure us that purgatorial time is radically different from our human computations of hours and minutes, years and weeks. We know nothing about it, say the theologians. Within the Roman Catholic system of indulgences, in which certain prayers are awarded an indulgence of, say, 300 days, this refers to the duration of an equivalent penance on earth, bearing no relation to the length of a purgatorial sojourn, which is indeterminate in terms of earthly time. The reincarnationist likewise would not presume to compute the length of the process by means of which we attain our moral goal. It may have already taken trillions of lives at various evolutionary stages to reach my present situation and trillions more may lie ahead of me. Some see only one reincarnation in store, and that only for an elect class.[7]

The tradition of the Greek Church has always been wisely disinclined towards neat systematisation in respect of the doctrine of purgatory, while the Roman Church, with its characteristic predilection for doctrinal definition, went further than could possibly be warranted, especially in relation to prayers and masses for the dead, a practice that plainly depends, of course, on a doctrine of the intermediate state. Yet it was not always so in the West. Ambrose, fourth-century Bishop of Milan whose preaching so impressed Augustine, affirmed simply that the souls of the departed await the end of time in a variety of habitations. Their fate, he taught, varied according to the quality of their works. Some were already with Christ. Others were waiting for presumably indeterminable periods. Augustine definitely taught a penal doctrine of purgatory.[8] Gregory the Great taught that one of the fundamental pains of purgatory is deprivation of the vision of God. (That deprivation, we must note, however, is part of our lot in this life, even for those who enjoy rare moments of foretaste of that bliss, in mystical ecstasy). Thomas Aquinas taught that the least of purgatorial pains is more terrible than the greatest pain on earth; nevertheless compared with hell it is a joyful and a peaceful state, since once you know you are in purgatory you know your salvation is assured. The souls in purgatory, according to this scholastic doctrine, are 'holy'. So, indeed, in Catholic devotion are they called: the 'Holy Souls'. They may be much helped by our prayers, which is not so with the souls in hell or even in limbo. By this time the extreme hardening of medieval purgatorial doctrine has taken place; yet even here the dynamic state of the Holy Souls is being taught. They are souls *in progress* towards the vision of God. The medieval Latin form of the doctrine, however distorted, also preserved a fundamental concept: the union between those on earth and those beyond the grave. Such as are still in the intermediate state can he helped by our prayers; such as have reached their final goal can help us.

If we look at the whole purgatorial tradition as dispassionately as possible, we shall see that the dominant note throughout it all is one of growth. Growth is painful. Older people talk glibly of the growing pains of childhood and adolescence, but unless we are already for all practical purposes at the end of life and ready for death we ought to be still suffering them. What we experience in this life is very much what is said to be the state of the

Holy Souls in purgatory: a mixture of anguish and struggle with
hope and of *joie de vivre*. Through the vale of tears we see the
heavenly vision. Are we talking, then, of this life or of purgatory?
Of both, since on the hypothesis I am proposing, this life is a phase
of the long purgatorial process. People sometimes say jocosely :
'Purgatory? I thought this is it!' I am suggesting that they may be
right. It is not the whole of it, but a slice. The more we seriously
entertain any notion of an afterlife the more, I think, we must
consider the possibility I am proposing.

Why, then, do we not remember earlier stages in our long
reincarnational pilgrimage? We shall be discussing at a later stage
some of the difficult problems such a question entails, such as what
we are to understand by the word 'I' in such a question. For the
moment let us consider an answer on a simpler level. Would not it
be better if I could go beyond my present brain cells that carry me
back to childhood memories into a memory of previous lives? Some
reincarnationists claim to be able to do just that, but for the
moment let us exclude them from our discussion.

Recalling past events in this life is both enjoyable and psychologically salutary. I happen to be one of those persons who is
able to recall with great clarity incidents from an extremely early
age. Mentally disturbed people are often helped through some
form of psychoanalysis to recall what they have hidden in the
unconscious, and this recalling can often be therapeutic.
Nevertheless, nothing is more merciful than our capacity to forget.
What if we remembered every sensation, every experience, every
thought, every event? The burden would soon become unbear-
able. As we advance in age we have accumulated, even in this
present life, an immense collection of memories. Even the liveliest
among us, by the time he or she has reached eighty or ninety, is not
expected to assimilate new ideas as easily as one did in one's youth.
The time comes when we need a fresh start. However vigorous my
body, however resilient my mind, my body does get more clogged
up and my mind more cluttered than was the case in earlier years. I
need to wipe my slate clean. Imagine what it would be like if I were
also saddled with such vivid memories of an earlier life. Worse still,
what if I could remember hundreds of previous lives, going back to
a life lived in, say, the Indus Valley before the writing of the
Upanishads and running through lives in Egypt and Greece, in
medieval Germany and Renaissance Italy, with perhaps an
occasional life on another planet intervening? The burden of such

a panorama of memories would be unendurable. It would so bog me down as to render me incapable of the further growth I need so much. One cannot profitably go on adding wood to the fire without ever cleaning out the ashes. Time comes when we must build a new fire. The purgatorial fire that burns all to dross, leaving only the gold, must be cleaned out from time to time. On the reincarnationist view that I am proposing as compatible with a Christian vision of human destiny, it would be cleared out at each death and rebirth, although, in some cases, vestigial memories of previous lives might remain. We shall return, in a later chapter, to a consideration of this possibility. Some reincarnationists claim extensive recollections of this kind. While I would counsel caution here, I shall provide later on at least one possible example out of my personal experience.

A reincarnationist interpretation of the purgatorial process does seem, then, in respect of the important points we have been considering, both plausible and remarkably well adapted to christening. Not only is it not incompatible with the traditional picture of purgatory, in so far as there is one; it makes the concept itself much more intelligible. Instead of seeing myself granted one life here on earth followed by another state in preparation for a final one, as is the traditional notion, I can see myself in the midst of a long evolutionary process, all of which is purgatorial in the sense that it is all part of the process by which I attain spiritual maturity.

There are two principal doctrines in Christian tradition on the origin of the human soul. According to the view called Creationism, God creates out of nothing a fresh soul for each human being at conception. This is the view upheld by Jerome and by Thomas Aquinas and other medieval Latin theologians. Thomas, following Peter Lombard,[9] taught that this is the Catholic doctrine and that any other is heretical.[10] This view was also generally accepted by the Calvinists. Some of the Fathers, however, upheld a different view, according to which the human soul is received by transmission from the parents. This other opinion, called Traducianism, was held by Gregory of Nyssa and by Tertullian, for example, and Augustine held a form of it. Lutheran theologians seem to have tended to be traducianist and some Roman Catholic theologians have revived Traducianism in modified forms. Antonio Rosmini-Serbati, a nineteenth-century Italian priest and thinker, founder of the Rosminians, a congregation of men and women, taught a modified form of it. He was suspect, however, of heresy on several counts.[11] In the history of Christian ideas Traducianism has some interest for us, because, while it can be expounded at a simple, materialistic level, as though the soul could be generated in the act of procreation, along with kidneys and spleen, some presentations of it do point to the evolution of the self, a notion that I think ought to be entertained today by those who seek an intelligible interpretation of human destiny in Christian terms.

If, as I am proposing, the individual is even now in the course of a long pilgrimage, it is possible to look back as well as forwards and to take stock of the life through which one is at present passing, giving it a slice in the long story of the individual's development. I, who have dreaded yet looked forward to this life, when it was in the future and appeared under the guise of a purgatory to come, am once again faced with another life, another step along the way, by means of which I may hope to advance in my grasp of the eternal verities. How, if at all, the process is to end is not our concern for the moment. What is suggested to me is that instead of a single, fleeting opportunity in terms of which my eternal destiny is to be for ever determined, I have already enjoyed, and shall have abundant further occasions for enjoying, unlimited opportunities to make myself what I know I ought to be.

That I am by no means alone in my struggles is a topic I do not wish to consider here, since it will be treated separately in another chapter. Suffice it to say that I am even less likely to be bereft of helpers under the arrangement I am suggesting than under the traditional view in which I am granted a guardian angel and encouraged to invoke the aid of other angels and saints to assist me along the way. In the concept I am proposing, such helpers would play a fundamental role and their capacity to help would be grounded no less in Jesus Christ. As we shall see when we come to the discussion of that aspect of the question, all who are in Christ will be understood to be active in helping their fellow pilgrims, whether in this life or beyond it. The help will be seen, moreover, as two-way: not only our prayers for those who have gone beyond into other struggles for development and growth but their prayers for us. Nor would that be changing the traditional scenario, since they would be praying for the 'souls in purgatory' as would we.

Dante's imagery presents a remarkably comprehensive grasp of the nature of the purgatorial process. Purgatory is a mountain, seven-storeyed, which all must ascend. Some spend longer on this or that storey, for each of the storeys symbolizes the purging of a particular warping of the soul, according to the medieval schema, which provided for seven 'capital', 'deadly' or fundamental sins that stand in the way of our vision of God. Pride, envy, anger, sloth, avarice, gluttony, lust: each evil is purged by the remedy best suited for its extirpation from the soul. On the first cornice, for example, the arrogant trudge, each bent low with the weight of a heavy load that he or she must carry. On the sixth, the gluttonous find themselves just out of reach of luscious fruit they long for. On the seventh, fire rages around those who in life enslaved themselves to their carnal lusts. At the summit of this penitential mountain is Eden, a terrestrial paradise whither Beatrice descends to meet Dante and to conduct him eventually through the various heavens. The whole of this part of the allegory of the *Commedia*, couched as it is in that beautiful medieval mixture of earthy images and ethereal symbolism, could stand as well for the model I am proposing as for any that have ever come within the ambit of standard Catholic tradition. The purgatorial dimension of spiritual evolution need no more be a mere 'second chance' than it need be a terraced mountain at the antipodes of Jerusalem. It is, rather, an aspect of what growth entails. If our nature as children of God be what the Bible and the Church have always accounted it, its fulfilment entails that purgatorial dimension. That is how we realize the spirituality of our nature. In the process we can never dispense with the body that is its instrument, yet we are continually transcending that which is at once our prison and our tool. Like the book from which we learn, it is nothing in itself, but through it we learn to be able to dispense with it and go on to another. As with that well-loved book, we cling to the body that has served us so well, even more when it has become tattered with use than when we got it in mint condition from the bookstore shelf. Yet, when the book eventually falls apart with use, we perceive, if we have learned its lesson well, that it has served its purpose and that our attachment to it is mere nostalgia which, however commendable in its way, must yield to the next book, the next stage in our growth, for which it, in turn, will be the instrument.

Consider a parallel from schooldays. Suppose you find you have a 'block' against a particular subject such as algebra, although you happen to be rather good at everything else. Algebra becomes your bugbear. You are soon the despair of your mathematics teacher, because without algebra you cannot hope to make headway in mathematics. Moreover, since some knowledge of mathematics is an essential part of one's general education, your whole school career may be in jeopardy. Either you must give up formal schooling altogether or else you must contrive somehow or other to overcome that hurdle, going back and back till you remove the block against algebra. Thereafter your academic progress is meteoric. So, then, it might be with rebirth. Some of us may have to spend numerous lives in narrow circumstances trying to learn something that is indispensable for further growth and that we fail, time after time, to master. The process would be tedious, but there would be no way around it. At last, however, when we do surmount the obstacle that has for so long held us back, we may make extraordinarily rapid progress, perhaps even taking one of those occasional, decisive leaps such as those that occur at the biological levels of the evolutionary process.

What bliss, after a long struggle on a hard road on which you seem to be making no headway at all, to find the road suddenly open out into a smooth path on which you can race like the wind! If it be so with rebirths, how urgent must be the need to succeed spiritually in that slice of our pilgrimage that is our present life, so as to avoid coming back for more and more of the same thing. That aspect of reincarnationism is seen even by those who in some oriental traditions look to it negatively as a way out of the tedium of life. In a Christian interpretation of reincarnationism, however, the emphasis would surely be on the fuller life that would ensue after such victory. Many of us have at least some faint foretaste of this kind of personal, moral triumph even here and now.

The interpretation of purgatory in reincarnational terms has obviously far-reaching consequences. Not only must we see the whole process of life and growth as purgatorial; the concept of purgatory, becoming more intelligible to us, loses any special terrors it might have. For if through Christian faith we can walk through this present life in the knowledge that Christ is upholding us all the way and that God's angels and saints watch benevolently over our every step, then that same faith will sustain us in whatever other lives lie ahead of us either here on this earth or even on any other planet. Fears diminish, even fade away. On our return the scenery may change, but the general conditions will not be radically different. So purgatory, as 'continual growth' in the 'love and service' of God becomes at least as acceptable to us as is the morrow of our present life. It becomes, indeed, no less than is heaven, a part of our Christian hope.

7 Evolution and the Concept of Reincarnation

The concept of evolution, set forth by Charles Darwin in his epoch-making work, *The Origin of Species*, and expounded by T. H. Huxley, Herbert Spencer, and others, was as revolutionary as had been the Copernican revolution in astronomy some four hundred years earlier. Indeed, in some ways it was even more far-reaching, radically affecting not only biology but virtually all important branches of human knowledge. By the turn of the century it had affected an *avant-garde* of theologians, represented by men such as Henry Drummond, James McCosh, John Fiske, Lyman Abbott and Minot Judson Savage. Fiske called evolution 'God's way of doing things' and McCosh wrote: 'Life seized the mineral mass, and formed the plant; sensation imparted to the plant made the animal; instinct has preserved the life and elevated it; intelligence has turned the animal into man; morality has raised the intelligence to love and law. The work of the spirit is not an anomaly. It is one of a series; the last and the highest. It is the grandest of all the powers. It is an inward power . . . preparing the soul for a heavenly rest, where . . . rest consists in holy and blessed service.[1] This remark, like others of the same period, sounds to many of us today almost as if it came from Teilhard de Chardin, although McCosh was writing when Teilhard was still a child.

Nevertheless, the full implications of evolutionism for Christian thought have not been adequately recognized even now, and those implications that have been noticed have not been always adequately worked out. For example, although twentieth-century process thinkers such as Teilhard have excited the minds of thoughtful Christians by showing how moral and spiritual concerns can fit an evolutionary anthropology, few Christian thinkers have given even the slightest attention to what this means for our attitude towards 'dumb' animals. Despite all that we have learned from an evolutionary understanding of the life process and especially of the development of man, we still work far too much from the now thoroughly outmoded assumption that man is a separately created species, fundamentally different from all other modes of life. That assumption is entirely unwarranted in the face of all we now know. Accepting it, consciously or unconsciously, cannot but vitiate all our thought about both the nature of man and the meaning of redemption by Christ.

That Christians in the ancient world accepted slavery as part of the social scenery, if not an inevitable element in the structure of human society, is well known. Nowadays that would be contrary to the conscience of almost all who profess Christianity. It would be accounted an intolerable affront to human dignity that even the lowest of men and women should be bred and sold like cattle. It is wrong, Christians generally would say, because we are all God's children, members of the Family of God, whether we know the grandeur of our heritage or not. When, however, similar questions are broached in respect of birds and beasts, the Church has almost nothing to say. We all admire Francis of Assisi and are touched by his love for all living creatures, but as far as Christian theology goes such thoughts are poetic conceits, not theological questions. Likewise we may applaud and may even encourage the work of humane societies that seek to protect horses and dogs and other 'dumb' animals from human cruelty; but Christian theology is silent. Some traditionally Christian countries, moreover, are notoriously cruel to animals. Robert Burton, in *The Anatomy of Melancholy*, noted that in the seventeenth century in which he lived England seemed a paradise for women but a hell for horses, while Italy looked a hell for women but a paradise for horses. Be that as it may, benevolent dispositions towards 'dumb' creatures, much as they may be widely lauded by individual Christians, are commonly supposed to spring from a humanitarian gentleness that is not at all uniquely Christian. Rightly so, for it would be difficult if not impossible to document a contention that they have some officially recognised Christian basis. Individual churchmen have occasionally uttered thoughtful sentiments about the destiny of animals. John Keble for instance, expressed a concern for the destiny of 'dumb creatures'; but I know of no official Church pronouncement on such questions. The 'lower creation' is generally dismissed as outside the scheme of salvation and is often contrasted with man as, in the traditional language of the English Book of Common Prayer, 'brute-beasts that have no understanding'.[2]

That this widespread attitude is still held can be shown from a report that comes to my desk even as I write. Lovers of Edinburgh know that, in 1858, a Skye terrier, Bobby, whose master had died, accompanied him to his grave in Greyfriars Churchyard and refused to move from the spot. He stayed there for many years, leaving it only for food at noontime and for shelter at night. When the dog himself eventually died after many years of this fidelity to his master's memory, admiring friends caused him to be buried beside his master. In time, a little fountain with a statue portraying Bobby was erected near the gates of the churchyard, becoming a much-loved tourist attraction, not to say place of pilgrimage. When, however, an attempt was made recently to have a plaque marking the site of Bobby's last resting place the proposal met official opposition. According to a city official, present-day legislation does not permit the burial of dogs in a cemetery for humans and if an exception were to be made, which would require special approval, careful use of tenses on the plaque would be required so as to make clear that the burial of Bobby had occurred before the present legislation.[3] The significance of official resistance to Bobby's being so commemorated is enhanced by the fact that Bobby has for many years enjoyed international posthumous fame. A very well-behaved dog might perhaps be admitted with his master to church for a special reason (I have known of such a case); but permanent interment in hallowed ground is another matter. What is most of all noteworthy about the case in point is that official opinion on the subject could be *even more* negative today than it was in Victorian times when the dog was in fact buried in the churchyard.

Few thoughtful Christians can feel at ease with the notion, deeply ingrained into traditional Christian thought, that such an absolute dichotomy ought to be made between human beings and their four-footed friends. For if we take the implications of evolution at all seriously, we cannot make any such sharp distinction between us and our ancestors. Within the human race itself is an enormous spectrum of development. 'The gulf that separates the highest animals from the lowest men is as nothing', wrote Savage, 'compared with the wider differences that lie between those lowest men and the Dantes, the Shakespeares and the Newtons of the race.'[4] On what grounds, then, can a Christian dare to set all horses, cat and dogs, including Greyfriars Bobby, on one side, while ranging moral and mental morons along with Schweitzer and Einstein and Mother Teresa on the other as two absolutely separate classes in the sight of God? It could be done only on the now outmoded dogmatic ground that the four-footed or 'dumb' animals are separate creations of God, contra-distinguished from man. This, we now know, cannot be the case. Great as was presumably the leap into the human condition, it cannot make us totally unrelated to the 'lower animals' as we could well seem to be when Adam could be accounted an entirely separate creation of God. I can no longer treat my cat as a separate species. She is my relative. If I may be said to have a 'soul', she must also be said to have at least an incipient 'soul'. If I am to be expected, as a Christian, to have a care for my less advanced brother man, why not for my dog or cat? The notion of putting them on anything like the same footing as a human being is still either shocking or odious to many Christians; but the only rationale for such an absolute distinction lies in the outmoded notion that man is a separate creation.

Reincarnationism, while it recognizes the enormous advance that has taken place in the evolutionary development we call humanity, can never make any such absolute distinction between man and his ancestors in the evolutionary tree. Reverence for life means reverence for all life, since my dog is as much my relative as is Neanderthal man. This need not injure this or that ecclesiology that sees me as in some way set apart by baptism. Yet we should not seek to justify an absolute dichotomy. What reincarnationism cannot allow is the notion that I dare treat non-human life as though it were totally separate from me and my human friends. In this, as in much else, a reincarnationist view accords with all that evolutionary biology has taught us during the past century and more. Reincarnationism and evolutionism are allies.

Nor should anyone suppose that the notion of evolution was really quite alien to Western thought even before Darwin's time. I have already briefly alluded to the concept of the superman (*hyperanthrōpos*) in early Christian thought. This notion and also the concept of deification through Christ that is to be found in some of the Greek Fathers developed out of the concepts of growth and transformation of human powers. We are developing towards the perfect man.[5].True, the ancients could not have seen evolution as having a biological background, as we must see it; nevertheless, some of them did see humanity as developing in such a way as to imply an evolutionary principle. Then, nearer modern times, Kant tells us that while he had followed with interest the events leading to the French Revolution of 1789, he hoped for the development of his own country by evolution, not by insurrection.[6] Franz von Baader, although he uses the concept of evolution as a category of history, not biology, does connect the history of man with the history of nature. He specifically connects evolution with the appearance of Christ in the historical form of Jesus, who has created a new element in the future of humanity. Jesus Christ, according to von Baader was not a revolutionary proposing the abolition of the Law but 'its evolutionary fulfilment'.[7] 'Christ', he says, 'fully possessed those treasures of God. But only very gradually did he display them before our eyes. He will progress steadily in this evolution, to the end of time, when he will again affirm man's reunion with God.[8] Not only does this early nineteenth-century German mode of thought prefigure, so far as could have been possible before the age of Darwin, the thought of Teilhard and other twentieth-century process thinkers; it accords with the Christian expectation of the redemptive process made possible by Christ: an expectation thoroughly rooted in New Testament teaching and plainly expounded by the Fathers of the Church.

After the expectation of the imminent return of Christ had waned, other ideas developed in which an element of progress in the soteriological process was seen. Even as early as the late second-century apocalyptic movement led by Montanus, this element can be detected. Here the notion of spiritual evolution comes under the guise of an age of redemption to be brought about by the Holy Spirit. No longer is humanity seen as about to come to an abrupt end; there is to be room for spiritual evolution, which takes time. In various forms, this concept appears from time to time in the Middle Ages. One of the most notable exponents of it was Joachim of Fiore, a twelfth-century mystic of whose life we know comparatively little. He is said to have experienced a conversion to a life of interiority while he was on a pilgrimage to the Holy Land, after which he entered a Cistercian monastery. Elected abbot against his will in 1177, he resigned office some years later in order to devote himself entirely to his writings. He founded a monastery of his own at Fiore, a village on the heights of the Sila mountains in Calabria. His foundation obtained papal approval in 1196, but his critical attitude towards the institutional aspects of the Church brought him, after his death, various ecclesiastical condemnations, for example, by the Fourth Lateran Council in 1215. The sanctity of his life was widely recognized and admired. Dante said of him that he was *di spirito profetico dotato*. He was indubitably a forerunner in some respects of the Franciscans and other thirteenth-century friars who made efforts to spiritualize the Church.

The concept of history that Joachim proposed definitely introduced a principle of development and progress. He conceives of history as having three periods: (1) the period of the Law, the *ordo conjugatorum*; (2) the period of Grace, the *ordo clericorum*; and (3) the period of the Spirit, the *ordo contemplantium*. Envisioning the rise of new orders in the Church that would bring about a new form of the Church, he even predicted a date for the beginning of the new age: the year 1260. In spite of the medieval and indeed pre-scholastic mode of Joachim's thought, the idea of progress and development that he presents is, for its time, definitely novel. He sees the realization of the ideal of the spiritual age as the emergence of a new kind of humanity, a humanity exalted to a superhuman dimension of being. Moreover, all this is to be accomplished not, as Augustine had proposed in his *De Civitate*, by the gradual overcoming of Babylon (the earthly City) by Jerusalem (the heavenly one, the Visible Church), but by the emergence of a new kind of man. Humanity is seen, not as a static species created once and for all by God in the Garden of Eden, but as a process making possible the emergence of transformed individuals.

Lord Monboddo, a remarkable Scottish judge writing in the eighteenth century (about 1757 to 1785), hit on the notion, apparently by an insightful guess, that man is related to the simians. People at that time were entirely ignorant of what fossils, for example, could reveal; yet Monboddo, in a stroke of genius, somehow anticipated the great discoveries of Darwin a century later. No doubt Monboddo, accounted by some an eccentric who proposed that man once had a tail, perceived in his own way the basic principle of both biological and moral evolution, though he lacked the scientific methodology the nineteenth century was to provide.[9]

Such bygone concepts of moral and spiritual evolution, in whatever guise they appear, are of interest as pointing in the direction of reincarnationist interpretations of human destiny. Once we introduce the notion of evolution of any kind, biological or moral, we are confronted by the vast magnitude of the process that any kind of evolution entails. We all know nowadays of the staggering antiquity of man. Born as we are into what we may call 'the space age,' we are by no means alien from our great-grandfathers who did not even know the bacteriological origin of many diseases. Nor were our ancestors in 'the Age of Reason' totally alien from the men of the Middle Ages. Nor again were the most primitive men entirely alien from their simian ancestors. In short, humanity is a process, not a species. It is a process of transition, over the course of millions of years. On the reincarnationist view, we have come a very long way and we have a very long way to go. We are pilgrims not merely for a few years but over the course of possibly trillions of lives. Like all pilgrims we are bespattered by the mud and covered with the dust of the road; like all pilgrims we know that we are on the way to ever greater and more exciting pilgrimages. Because we are pilgrims we are never entirely at home.

Church teaching has always portrayed us as pilgrims, yet it has rarely carried the notion to its logical end, which (if only for the reasons that Kant perceived) must be beyond the present life. Whatever we may think of reincarnationism, the notion that we reap what we sow and that the process must take a very long time does appeal to all who, for one reason or another, believe, as did Kant, that there is a moral principle or agent at the core of the universe. Once that is granted, something such as Kant's postulates follows, although not necessarily in precisely the way in which he formulated them two centuries ago. I must have the capacity to do whatever I am certain that I ought to do. If I ought, I can. But the life of the world to come, as far as it can be portrayed in the confusion traditionally attending Church teaching on the subject, provides no way of fulfilling duties unfulfilled in the present life. For if purgatory is a mere penitentiary and heaven unmitigated bliss, the fulfilment of duties lies outside their scope. If I have anything at all like a Kantian conscience, reincarnationism seems to fit the case peculiarly well.

Kant himself, in an early paper published in 1755, the year he became a Privatdozent at the University of Königsberg, speculated that the immortal soul may travel, in the course of an infinity of time, from one planet to another.. 'Who knows,' he asks, 'but that the intention is that it should become acquainted at close range sometime with those distant globes of the cosmic system and the excellent institutions they may have, which already provoke our curiosity? Perhaps it is just for such a purpose that some globes in the planetary system are in a preparatory state, ready to become a new habitation for us when we have completed the time of our stay here. Who knows but that Jupiter's satellites may some day shine on us?'[10] Although in some of his later work he dissociated himself from 'fantastical theosophic dreams', there is some evidence that in lectures he was giving on the eve of the publication of the *Critique of Pure Reason* in 1781 he taught the pre-existence of the soul. It is also known from his posthumous works that in his later years he was moving in a Spinozistic direction.

Our main point here is that, given Kant's fundamental position on the nature of man and his moral consciousness, together with the Age of Reason in which he lived and his comparative freedom from ecclesiastical control, he could not easily have been unattracted to reincarnationism in one form or another, at least as an interesting speculation. His speculation about the continuation of life on other planets must have seemed much wilder, not to say more academically disreputable, in his time (when the possibility of a trip even to the moon was unthinkable) than it would be for us today.

Although Kant, writing a century before Darwin, could not have had our perspective on biological evolution, he was, as a moral evolutionist, able to speculate at least on the consequences of such a position for man's future as well as for his past. The *summum bonum*, which is the object of the moral law, entails for its realization an endless moral progress. He could see the danger in those false neo-Gnostic systems that pretend to secure for their initiates some sort of instant deification, making moral evolution unnecessary. All such antinomianism, neo-Gnostic or not, purports to dispense with Law. That is fundamentally opposed to the New Testament witness and the teaching of Jesus himself as recorded in the Gospels.

Now that we know something of the astounding sweep and complexity of the evolution of life from its simplest forms to the most highly organized ones, we are in a better position to appreciate the immensity of any moral evolutionism such as Kant's.

If it takes many millions of years for vertebrates to evolve and many millions more to produce the half-bestial, half-angelic biped we call man, how long does it take to fulfil the now merely incipient capacities of this most astonishing of all living entities that are empirically perceptible? To how many accidents must not he be prone in the course of his moral development? Then when we reflect on the enormous differences to be found in the development of individual human beings, to which allusion has already been made earlier in the present chapter, the notion that our entire destiny could be determined in the course of one little span of years becomes almost unintelligible, except on the positivistic supposition that the individual has no destiny other than the grave, which is of course a supposition antithetical to *all* Christian hope. Nor can the process of moral evolution begin abruptly with the attainment of an upright gait; it must have a long antecedent history, bringing the whole animal kingdom within our moral concern and making any restriction of that concern to humans a deplorably parochial proceeding.

Acute awareness of that moral truth came to Albert Schweitzer suddenly.He had been thinking of ethical questions for some months and had found traditional conceptions 'so lifeless, so unelemental, so narrow and so destitute of content that it was quite impossible to bring them into union with the affirmative attitude' to life that he felt must be maintained. He was sure that there must be an inner connection between that affirmative attitude and ethics, but nothing he had learned enabled him to make the connection. Then one day in the course of a rather long river trip, as his boat was making its way through a herd of hippopotamuses at sunset, a phrase suddenly came into his mind, expressing the connection he sought: *reverence for life*. He goes on to say: 'The great fault of all ethics hitherto has been that they believed themselves to have to deal only with the relations of man to man. In reality, however, the question is what is his attitude to the world and all life that comes within his reach. A man is ethical only when life, as such, is sacred to him, that of plants and animals as that of his fellow men, and when he devotes himself helpfully to all life that is in need of help. . . . The ethic of the relation of man to man . . . is only a particular relation which results from the universal one.'[11] Schweitzer, in making this leap beyond traditional ethics, exhibits his extraordinary genius by perceiving, under that comprehensive phrase, what had been fundamentally wrong with the development of ethical thought that Christianity had inherited and elaborated. By restricting ethics to human relations, human duties and human rights, Christian thought had distorted the nature of the spiritual quest. It was as if one were to restrict the possibility of education to one's university years taking account neither of kindergarten nor of what one learns in later years in 'the school of life'.

Schweitzer was much interested in and disposed to the concept of reincarnation, so far as he understood it in Indian thought. He wrote of it as surmounting 'difficulties which baffle the thinkers of Europe. . . . If we assume that we have but one existence, there arises the insoluble problem of what becomes of the spiritual ego which has lost all contact with the Eternal. Those who hold the doctrine of reincarnation are faced by no such problem. For them that non-spiritual attitude only means that those men and women have not yet attained to the purified form of existence in which they are capable of knowing the truth and translating it into action.'[12] When he was persuaded to visit the United States on the occasion of the Goethe bicentenary celebrations, he was greeted at the dockside by a battery of cameras and reporters. Bowing to them he said in French: 'Ladies and gentlemen, in my youth I was a stupid young man. I learned German and French, Latin, Greek, Hebrew — but no English. In my next incarnation, English shall be my first language.'[13] The idea of reincarnation, alien as it must have seemed to Schweitzer from the mainstream of Christian thought, could not fail to fascinate one who had hit upon 'reverence for life' as the basic principle of moral evolution.

Christian orthodoxy demands that God must be conceived as standing beyond the evolutionary process. Schemes such as those of Samuel Alexander and Henry Nelson Wieman, for example, interesting though they be to metaphysical philosophers, do not conform to this requirement; those of William Temple, Pierre Teilhard de Chardin and Lionel Thornton do. Christian orthodoxy, in contrast to Judaism and Islam, must find a place for Christ who, as divine Being, enters in some way into the stream of humanity and into the redemptive process.

Reincarnation, in its traditional form, is, as we have seen, very much a moral-law concept. So of course it can be shown to correspond on that score to the moral principles that the Christian Way has inherited and has always sought to encompass. But what of the grace of Christ? What of angels and saints and other helpers?

How can the rigorous karmic law that developed forms of reincarnationism presuppose accommodate what is most distinctive in Christian faith: the fact that 'we have no power of ourselves to help ourselves'? In our next chapter I shall hope to show how such concepts do fit a reincarnational scheme.

8 Angels and Other Ministers of the Grace of God

Angels and ministers of grace defend us!
Shakespeare, *Hamlet*

The concept of angels and other divine emissaries whose functions include helping humans is ancient and widespread in the major religions of the world. In Mahayana Buddhist tradition, for instance, the bodhisattvas (buddhas-to-be) function somewhat like angels. In the monotheistic religions, however (Judaism, Christianity, Islam), the role of angels has a special history. In Judaism the gulf between God and man is so great that angels (messengers) or the like seem indispensable as a bridge of communication. The Old Testament has many allusions to them. In the Wisdom literature some of them are named; for example, Michael, Gabriel, and Raphael. Islam, in the same Semitic tradition, has a similarly obvious need, represented in a strong tradition of the same sort. Angels are supposed to be present at the public recitation of prayers in the mosque. Devout Muslims, at the end of the prayers, greet them with a bow to the left and to the right.

Christianity inherited this characterisitcally Semitic traditon and expressed it in early documents of the faith. When God announced to Mary that she was to bear Jesus, he did so through the agency of Gabriel.[1] In the Apocalypse we read of war in heaven in which Michael and the angels engage in combat with the Evil one and his wicked angels.[2] In Matthew we read that Jesus himself, when one of his followers had tried to intervene at his arrest by striking the high priest's servant, rebuked the impetuous disciple with the reminder that God, if asked, would promptly send twelve legions of angels' to defend him.[3] Even Jesus, then, entertained the possibility of angelic help.

In the mystical tradition that has as its focus the Pseudo-Dionysius who flourished about AD 500, we find the angelic hosts hierarchically arranged in three orders, with three choirs in each. In descending order they are: (1) seraphim, cherubim, thrones; (2) dominations, virtues, powers; and (3) principalities, archangels, angels. Angels and archangels are the choirs principally charged with missions to human beings. This arrangement, although in part indebted to Scripture, was plainly speculative. The thirteenth-century schoolmen took it over and developed it. In the thought of Thomas Aquinas, angels play a singularly important role.

The notion of guardian angels, each specially charged with guiding and protecting a particular human being, is specifically taught in the *Shepherd* of Hermas, an important second-century Christian writing.[4] This belief was common in the ancient world, being found, for instance, in Plato.[5] It appears in popular Roman religion in the notion of the Genius who guides every man and the Juno who guides every woman. It is also found in Enoch and there are traces of it in the canonical Old Testamemt literature. Later Christian opinion is expressed in a variety of attitudes. Ambrose, for instance, suggests the interesting notion that saintly people are deprived of guardian angels so that, having to struggle alone, they grow greater in spiritual strength.[6] In popular Catholic devotion, angels have continued to play a part; but it tends to be overshadowed by that of the saints, the heroes of the Church who have gone before us and whose aid we enlist in prayer.

For our purposes the important point here is that the notion of unseen helpers and protectors is beyond all doubt both indigenous to early Christian thought and practice and a lively element in traditional Catholic devotion. All this accords with a very ancient gnostic and theosophical outlook in which unseen helpers, by whatever name they may be called, play an immense role. Its importance arises from the concept, very strong in these traditions and certainly present in the mainstream of Christian thought, that evil agencies stand all around us, ever threatening to injure and if possible destroy us.

All New Testament teaching presupposes that we are beset by such evil powers. Not only, as we are dramatically reminded in the Office of Compline, is our 'enemy the devil prowling around like a roaring lion looking for someone to eat';[7] evil agencies are ever busy working in all sorts of subtle ways for our destruction. As Paul Tillich constantly reminded his audiences, demonic powers rule the world. This is an ancient and specifically Gnostic notion. As Christians, the higher we go the more persistently will these evil agencies work for our undoing. This is a point masterfully popularized by C.S. Lewis in his perspicacious modern classic *The Screwtape Letters*. Evil powers are less likely to be interested in us when we are small fry than when we might seem worth the catch. Hence their ferocity in attacking those who are well advanced on the path of spirituality. All this is standard Christian teaching and it accords very much with the traditions in which reincarnationism is most at home. Our pilgrimage entails a constant war with these evil agencies. Christians as diverse in background and outlook as Ignatius of Loyola and John Bunyan testify to that. We must not underestimate the fearful power of these demonic forces that we see both in our interior lives and in the power dynamics of the political scene. They can ensnare, mislead, beguile, seduce and eventually destroy us. Hence the scriptural admonition: 'Stand up to him, strong in faith and in the knowledge that your brothers all over the world are suffering the same things'.[8] One of the chief functions of prayer is to protect us from these destructive agencies. If there were no such agencies much of our prayer would be as unnecessary as would be preventive medicine in a world devoid of viruses and bacteria harmful to human health.

No less characteristically Christian is the teaching that against such foes we should be utterly helpless but for the power of Christ ever undergirding us. According to all Christian teaching, any sense of salvation that we may enjoy, any assurance we may have of having been 'written in the Book of Life', is unthinkable apart from the Person and work of Jesus Christ. Apart from him we are helpless; for we have 'no power of ourselves to help ourselves'. Christ makes salvation possible by providing the indispensable conditions for it. Yet in working out our salvation 'in fear and trembling' as Scripture enjoins,[9] we need all the help we can get in appropriating the 'amazing grace' of Christ. So, then, Christians learn from experience to be grateful for whatever protection or guidance they may receive from the unseen helpers that they find attending them.

Many parapsychologists believe there is evidence of one kind or another for the presence around us of invisible agencies. If, as is well established, a parent or husband or wife in one part of our planet can reach out in an emergency with spiritual support to a beloved person at the antipodes, why should not we be guarded or

helped by invisible agencies at a more advanced state of
consciousness than our own? Some persons have a highly developed
awareness of such help. Some of these claim to know whence it
comes; others make no such claim. Some Christians, recognizing
the phenomenon, may prefer to label it under the general category
of Providence. What is important is that well-disciplined,
resourceful Christians who are thoroughly inured to the inner life
of prayer are so accustomed to the phenomenon that, whatever
language they use, they can have no reason to look askance at those
whose language is different but whose claims are substantially the
same as their own.

The notion of an 'inner voice' is, despite its noble lineage in the
Stoic background of Roman Law, rightly suspect. It is certainly
not on that alone that one should base the sort of claim we are
considering here. The evidence presents itself more characteristically in a complex of circumstances (sometimes in an unusual
turn of events not easily accounted for, sometimes in the
unaccountable development of the complex of circumstances) that
somehow stays our hand from what we later see would have been
disastrous. Or else it leads us towards an unexpected opportunity.
Our attribution of it to Providence is, of course, an interpretation:
one that many onlookers would not allow, but one that we may
find fitting the case better than any other we know. From such a
typical attitude on the part of devout Christians of many different
traditions the step to the notion of invisible realms of helpers
constantly watching over us, not interfering with our freedom but
guiding our feet along the way, cannot be difficult and should not
be alarming.

We need not be reminded, in such an age of psychologism, that
the evils that rise up to destroy us are in ourselves, possibly hidden
deep in our psyche. The question is always: how did they get there
in the first place? We permitted evil and destructive thoughts to
enter into us and issue in the neuroses and other psychic fungi that
hurt us and impede our creativity and growth. The virus is indeed
in us; but we let it in by our invitation or at least by our carelessly
leaving the door open. No Christian should boggle at such notions,
for they are written into the heart of what Scripture has to say on
the subject, whatever be the kind of language we may choose to
employ in describing the situation. That the war between good
and evil is ever at our doorstep and that we are part of the dis-
puted terrain is a familiar theme to all thoughtful Christians.

Reincarnationists, however they may express the situation, are peculiarly aware of the phenomena.

The very reliance of Christians on the supremely effective power of Christ in combatting these evil agencies would be proof, were one needed, of the Christian's intense awareness of the reality of these demonic powers. The Christian may put the fullest reliance in Christ's power yet recognize also the Christian responsibility to enlist help. The fact that God has given 'his angels charge over thee, to keep thee in all thy ways . . . lest thou dash thy foot against a stone',[10] should not blind us to the injunction, quoted by Jesus in his encounter with Satan: 'Ye shall not tempt the Lord your God.'[11] It was when this encounter had ended and the devil had left that 'angels came and ministered unto him.'[12] All this is characteristic of the gnostic climate of thought in which Christianity was cradled and in which reincarnational concepts are indigenous. When we Christians, who acknowledge Jesus Christ as our Lord and Saviour, learn from the Gospel narratives that he received and accepted the ministrations of angels, surely we must go on to acknowledge how inadequately we have appropriated the riches of this part of our Christian heritage. Ought not the notion of invisible helpers from other dimensions of being play a much larger part than it does in the outlook of many of us?

Also deeply etched into Christian liturgy is the notion, particularly celebrated in the Feast of All Saints, that we are 'compassed about with so great a cloud of witnesses[13] that we, as Christians, can never account ourselves entirely alone. These 'witnesses' are not only the 'angels and archangels' with whom we declare ourselves joined in every celebration of the Eucharist but the men and women who have gone before us in faith and have passed beyond the state of our present pilgrimage. We may speculate, if we will, that they, or some of them, may have been already reincarnated on other planets, for example; but what is more to the point is the notion that, wherever they are and whatever the state of their being, they are able, through the bond that binds all Christians in the Body of Christ, to help us along a path that is thornier than we can know.

The reincarnationist would go on to say that even in human relationships here and now the friends we have known in previous lives sometimes turn up to help us in other ways in our struggles. In a truly happy marriage, for instance, one may be re-encountering a 'soul-mate' from the past. Casual acquaintances or even excitingly interesting friends may be new to us and, as we sometimes may say, like ships that pass in the night; but certain friendships and associations, of which a happy marriage is but a striking example, are so deeply influential on our lives that we may feel they have been 'sent' to us as part of the equipment of our present pilgrimage. The old saying that 'marriages are made in heaven' reflects such ancient reincarnational insights. Although notions of that sort are superficially alien to traditional Christian theology and the official teachings of the Church, popular Christian sentiment has been at least to some extent hospitable to them and many mature Christians of independent mind have for long cherished them. I do not see that they should be accounted alien to any fundamental Christian attitude or belief.

Serious Christian discussion of the nature of prayer is relevant to the question now before us. For prayer does present notoriously difficult theological problems and, since it is at the heart of all Christian life (both the life of the individual and the life of the Church), these problems cannot be ignored by any thoughtful person. Very general, if not universal, in the practice of all the great religions of the world, prayer is intellectually puzzling. Unbelievers find prayer, especially petitionary prayer, in which the petitioner asks for a specific grace or favour, an easy butt of their ridicule. Here on one side of an old battle line was the Lutheran chaplain invoking divine aid to kill the British, while the Anglican chaplain on the other side was no less earnestly supplicating the defeat of the Germans. On what basis is God to choose between the petitioners? Whose request is he to grant? My business competitor prays for his own success, which might well ruin me, while I pray for the success I need for my family's support, which might ruin him. Even intercessory prayer presents difficulties. You tell me that your sister is dying, so I, being your devoted friend, pray earnestly for her recovery, unaware that you, who know the situation better than I, pray even more earnestly for her death which you believe with excellent reason to be best for her. Seen from such standpoints the whole practice of prayer can be made to seem both silly and futile.

Behind the practice of prayer, however, is a much deeper significance and purpose. In prayer we can generate more powerful psychic energy than is possible by any other means. In view of what we now know of telepathic phenomena, we can see that through prayer, as an act of intense love, we can exert immense influence for good. This is true of even the feeblest kinds of prayer; it is superabundantly true of great prayer. Alexis Carrel, a Nobel Laureate in medicine, claims to have seen a malignant tumour shrivel at Lourdes under the influence of prayer.

We have seen in an earlier chapter that, on any reincarnationist view, spiritual evolution is a long and arduous process. An individual may fail, as did at the biological level the dinosaur and the dodo. That is what gives such special significance to one form of Christian belief, so much stressed by some heirs of the Reformation tradition, that the Christian has reached a stage in which he enjoys the 'blessed assurance' that, however long the process may still be in his or her case, ultimate victory is assured. A plateau in spiritual evolution has been reached and there is no going back. Others, however, more impressed by the virulence of evil, see the battle increasing in intensity as higher and higher stages are attained. What concerns us here is that surely no thoughtful Christian need be astonished at the notion that prayer assists in the evolutionary process. It is what seems to be presupposed in Christian practice, whatever traditional theology may say about it.

Our prayers to the invisible helpers are in two directions: (1) we invoke their aid for ourselves, and (2) we ask for it on behalf of others, notably, in Catholic practice, on behalf of those who have gone before us and may much need our prayers in the intermediate state traditionally called purgatory. Prayer always presupposes a two-way traffic. Whatever it is, it is not narcissistic luxuriatings or a do-it-yourself catharsis; it is always action that presupposes the transmission of psychic energy and power. The Christian, we need hardly remind ourselves, will always see God as the source of that power; but saints and others advanced in the pilgrimage of the spirit can and do transmit the energy to us, while we can also transmit it to some who need our help. The whole process we call prayer can then be seen as the manifestation of the power of love, the love that conquers all.

Origen, whose importance we have already considered, wrote a great treatise on prayer. After discussing the need to choose a suitable place for it, he goes on to say that 'it may be, angelic powers also stand by the gatherings of believers, and the power of the Lord and Saviour himself, and holy spirits as well, those who have fallen asleep before us. . . .'[14] He also suggests that at assemblies of the faithful each individual has his or her guardian angel present so that, as he quaintly puts it, there is 'a double Church, the one of men, the other of angels.' Here Origen exhibits the principle I am suggesting as an authentic philosophy of prayer for those Christians who, while remaining faithful to the basic tenets of traditional Christian faith, seek to see these tenets in the light of an evolutionary understanding of the pilgrimage that is to take us into 'the life of the world to come'.

Catholic practice recognizes levels of prayer. The formulae of vocal prayer (for example, the *Pater noster*, the *Ave Maria*), are useful as backdrop for what the Church hopes may be (as in the popular devotion of the rosary) the more contemplative and meditative kinds of prayer that are prescribed as a descant upon the familiar words. True, the rosary can very easily degenerate, as the prayer-wheel in certain forms of Buddhism degenerated, into a mere mumble; but this happens to all sorts of prayer. For in prayer, as in economics, a sort of Gresham's Law operates: as bad money drives out good, so cheap prayer tends to drive out the costliest kind, the kind that entails sacrificial love. Yet the fact that in popular devotions such as the rosary the Church recognizes such levels of devotion and that they can operate in the same person at the same time shows the wisdom behind Catholic instinct: a recognition that, although not all prayer is equal in spiritual value, all may be used in the tremendous work that is the advancement of humankind towards its goal.

The highest form of prayer, according to the testimony of the great saints of the Church, is the kind that leads to mystical union with God. It is also recognized by Thomas Aquinas and others to be the most dangerous. For it may easily lead to pretentious humbug and worse. Yet the fact, only too well known, is that all religion stands in the same condemnation, not least Christianity. That is not to say that we should despise or reject what can be a ladder to heaven. Charlatans abound in all fields of human enterprise. Surely it goes without saying that that need be no reason for discouragement in any human undertaking and certainly by no means so in our attempts, however feeble, to listen to the song of the angels.

9 Memory and Claims of Recollection of Previous Lives

> I remember, I remember
> The house where I was born,
> The little window where the sun
> Came peeping in at morn.
>
> Thomas Hood, *I remember, I remember*

> The waves came shining up the sands,
> As here to-day they shine;
> And in my pre-pelasgian hands
> The sand was warm and fine.
>
> Frances Cornford, *Pre-existence*

Nothing is more central to Christian faith and hope than the belief and expectation that through the power of Christ we, too, shall rise after death and sooner or later assume a new and more 'glorious' body. This resurrection body, however 'glorified', is to stand in the same relation to 'me' as does my present one. Such is the universal testimony of the mainstream of Christian orthodoxy and clearly follows Paul's teaching. Both death and resurrection are realities for the Christian.

We need not speculate (Paul indeed discourages us from such speculation) on what sort of 'brain' such a 'glorified' resurrection body will include. Nevertheless, whatever it is it must surely include the power to recall at least something of what has been imprinted on my brain in the present life. Of course one would not expect to remember all; I recall much less than that as things are. Since, in spite of my having extremely clear recollections of very early childhood, I cannot remember, for instance, the telephone number of the house I lived in twenty years ago, I certainly should not expect to remember such trivia in my future 'glorified' state. But surely I shall recall some things out of this present life, this vale

99

of tears, this scene of my redemption by Christ. Otherwise, how should I even know to praise God for having so redeemed me? If I knew nothing of the pilgrimage that had preceded my glorified state, how could I know of my having been, as Wesley put it, 'snatched like a brand from the burning', the recipient of God's 'amazing grace'? The grander the cerebral equipment (or its counterpart) in my resurrection body, compared with the feebler instrument of the present one, the more monstrous the notion that it might not carry over from the present one, with some clarity and distinctness, at least some recollections of my present life.

In fact, of course, a remarkably large number of churchgoers, in their perplexity over the concept of resurrection and its entail-ments, have simply abandoned belief in personal survival, their liturgical affirmations at the singing of the Creed notwithstand-ing. There is, however, no way in which such a person can be accounted a Christian, even on the most heterodox or 'liberal' reckoning. Christian faith bereft of Christian hope is foolish and futile. If there be any single belief apart from which Christianity totters and falls lifeless, it is belief in resurrection, an implicate of which is continuity between this life and that of the world to come. Although this obvious implicate of the Christian hope has been largely ignored in traditional theology, we find an expression of it in the widely popular expectation that we shall recognize our friends 'on the other shore' and be recognized by them. What is abundantly clear is that a resurrected body such as is envisioned in Christian hope would be unthinkable apart from some memory of the present life.

I wish to establish this at the outset of any discussion of the possibility of recollection of previous lives such as many rein-carnationists claim to enjoy. For whatever difficulties, philo-sophical and scientific, attend the notion of recollections of previous lives attend no less every Christian's basic hope for the life of the world to come. The problem is by no means the reincarnationist's only. Every Christian faces it, knowing that he or she must carry over at least some awareness of the present life. The early Fathers and Church Councils perceived in their own way the need for such continuity (antiquated as their concepts may seem to us) when they insisted that it is the same body, 'the body we now have', that is to be resurrected. The notion, in that form, cannot but be unacceptable to us today in the light of all we know. But although we cannot suppose of course, that the now ever-changing cells of the body are to be re-assembled and enhanced as our distant forefathers might have supposed, Christians are still most certainly committed to some continuity of memory transmitted from the focus of consciousness within the present body to the focus of consciousness in the 'glorified' one. That is precisely the problem that confronts every reincarnationist.

It is certainly a formidable one. Claims such as many reincarnationists make of recalling incidents and situations, some of them in detail, elicit skepticism in the minds of most people, even the least critical. Most empirical philosophers today would account claims to any such recollections nonsensical and their exploration therefore futile. Not only do our brains stop functioning at death; in some cases we can observe in others the process of deterioration from advancing senescence to the eventual total cessation of all functioning. Even if one were to grant the hypothesis (general among reincarnationists) of an 'etheric double' or field of energy that might store certain memories in such a way as to enable them to be transmitted from one of my embodiments to another, or from my present body to a resurrection one, how could the new body's brain (or its equivalent) recapture and provide recollections from a previous life in which a different brain had been functioning? What sort of memory could it be that could be seen to fail in extreme old age and then be somehow restored and emerge again in another brain? The fact that in a senescent brain powers of memory for recent events may often diminish while memory of much more distant ones remains unimpaired might perhaps have some relevance to the problem before us; nevertheless, a fundamental problem remains.

It was expressed long ago by Charles Richet, Professor of Physiology in the University of Paris, a Nobel Laureate in 1913, and a President of the Society for Psychical Research. Richet, while immensely interested in the notion of life after death and much impressed by the work of F.W.H. Myers and Sir Oliver Lodge, maintained an attitude of professional skepticism. He recognized that 'innumerable facts have proved that memory is a function that very soon disappears, that asphyxia, anaemia and poisons impair it immediately; it is extremely frail; it diminishes rapidly with advancing age.' He goes on to point out: 'To survive without remembrance of the old Self is not to survive at all.'[1] There is the nub of the problem as it was seen at a comparatively early stage in the history of modern psychical research. Memory alters and disappears when the supply of oxygen is cut off, when the course of cerebral irrigation is stopped, or even when a little atropine or morphine is introduced into the blood. So little is needed to enfeeble and erase memory. Even if we indulge in the very theoretical postulate that I could have a successful brain transplant that would restore to me the power of memory, as a function of my 'new brain', we must presume that nevertheless all my recollections up to that point would have been irrevocably lost, as surely as if I had discarded an old computer and were using a new one.

That the brain functions as does a computer is well known. True, its operations are extremely complex and neurophysiologists recognize that knowledge of the brain and its potentialities is still very limited. Nevertheless, it does have a computer function and this function accounts for what we generally understand as memory: my recollection, for instance, of the contents of my desk drawer, your telephone number, and the city in which I lived thirty years ago. That the brain functions as a computer in respect of *such* memory seems obvious. When we look, however, at other kinds or aspects of memory such as what Bergson called 'habit-memory', the analogy seems less clearly apposite, to say the least.[2] Were I to say to you, 'Try to remember to wake up tomorrow morning, will you?' you would probably take it as a joke. For waking up in the morning is not something that you try not to forget to do as you try not to forget your daughter's birthday. You do not put a note in your calendar or a knot in your handkerchief; you know you will wake up, for you do it, as we say, by instinct, not special programming. Nor do you leave an alcoholic with a bottle of Scotch at his side and tell him to be sure not to forget to have a drink. He will have one before he is even aware of having it and may well finish the bottle. We can hardly say he has been 'programmed' to take a drink whenever he has the opportunity. We say, rather, that he has 'fallen into the habit', or even that it has become 'second nature' to him. Some sort of memory is involved in such instinctive actions, but it is not the sort by means of which I commit your telephone number 'to memory' and accurately recall it, which takes an act of careful programming.

Again, in dreams I call upon the store of my memory. I dream about you or your house or a dragon I have seen in a picture book and often, of course, about images whose origins I cannot identify so easily, if at all. That, too, is a very different operation from, say, what a lawyer does in assembling the salient points of a case he is to cite next morning in court. In dreams, although the images do not come in altogether higgledy-piggledy but, rather, according to a pattern of their own that makes sense in its own way (as does science fiction), they do not come in as programmed by a computer. A computer might serve me for recording dreams I have dreamed, but not for dreaming them. It could even help me in writing a novel or a play and certainly in business enterprises, but it can no more do business creatively than it can write an original novel.

We shall return to dreams later in this chapter. Psychoanalysts claim to find in them clues to neuroses and pointers to their cure. Perhaps not only dreams reveal our past. Plato, in his well-known story in the *Meno*, tells of an intelligent slave who could pick up and grasp a geometrical theorem very quickly because, according to Plato, he had learned it in a previous life. That is at any rate a way of saying that when we have an aptitude for a subject we do not have to go through laborious operations to understand what the book or teacher says. We know it already. A mathematical prodigy does not have to learn the multiplication table like the rest of us, nor does he need reasons to arrive at his conclusions. It is *as if* he had learned all that long ago and needed only to recall it, as I might be able to recall your name after not seeing you for some years, though only if I had liked you or found you interesting. Once we *master* anything, such as playing the piano or even riding a bicycle, we may get out of practice, but, as we say, 'it soon comes back to us'.

Before we broach the question of how much and what kind of memory we might need to establish the continuity that Christian faith implies between my awareness in this life and my awareness in the life of the world to come, let us consider some aspects of memory as it occurs in our present experience, ignoring for the moment all claims to memory of previous lives such as some reincarnationists make.

Memories of childhood vary from individual to individual both in intensity and extent. To those who can recall nothing very distinctly before the age of ten, even the modest claims of those who say they can clearly remember incidents that occurred at four or five may seem far-fetched, while the claims of those who say they can recall from as early as two or three may seem suspect. I do not mean that they may be suspected of intentional fabrication, only that the claimants imagine they recall what has been in fact recounted to them years after the event.

Since I happen to be among those who recall with great clarity and distinctness experiences from an extremely early age, I have for long been interested in the problem of authenticating such claims. I do not feel the slightest need to authenticate them for my own satisfaction and I shall presently show why I am subjectively so confident; but I am well aware of the nature of the objection.

Plainly, all forms of reporting are and ought to be subject to searching criticism; that is why intelligent people generally try to read more than one newspaper. Autobiography, however, is more than ordinarily suspect, even your report of what happened to you yesterday. I have no reason to question your integrity or the honesty of your intentions; nevertheless, I have a right to raise the obvious question: is not your account inevitably tainted with subjectivity, to say the least, and therefore cannot be entirely trusted? If that is true of what you tell me of yesterday's happening, how much more suspect are you when you claim to be reporting to me such distant occurrences as your early childhood? Is not it likely that your mother, when you were ten or eleven, told you of a place you lived in or a dog you loved at the age of three, and that you then fancied you actually remembered that house or that dog? It is not that you are charged with trying to deceive me, only that you may be deceiving yourself. Nevertheless, if I do want to learn about you, your feelings and your thoughts, where else shall I go? You are the best possible authority, at least from one very important point of view. So autobiography, for all its shortcomings, is one of the most fascinating of art forms, perhaps even the supreme literary form. The letters of great men and women are similarly fascinating, because they exhibit their writers as they see themselves. So I still want to hear your report of yourself, since it alone can be first hand. Yet the problem of authentication remains.

My interest in this question has led me to perceive that there is at any rate a simple subjective test. Let us consider that first. The feeling tone of an experience at the age of three is radically different from the feeling tone of an experience at eight or twelve. In very early childhood, experiences come with a vivacity that is uncharacteristic of later life. Colours, for instance, are breathtaking, even painfully vivid. I have one recollection that I can date from external circumstances to within about a month, when I was nineteen months old. It includes the stone floor of a farmhouse kitchen and a field of red poppies. Never since have I experienced anything like the intensity of the colours. The only descriptions I have heard that convey anything of it are from accounts of what people have experienced under the influence of LSD or other drugs with which I have never experimented. I know from recollections of experiences dating from the age of three or four that even by then I should have been absolutely incapable of perceiving anything like that colour intensity. I know that nobody could conceivably have told me about colour intensity of that kind in later childhood, for nobody who would be reflecting on it would have been talking to me about it, even in my later childhood. I remember also, as an only child who in early years almost never met a non-adult, my extreme sense of singularity.

The helplessness and ignorance peculiar to very early childhood give another special dimension to recollections of it. Even by the age of seven my experience as I recall it is permeated with a degree of criticism, however modest, and a considerable sense of power such as simply were not there at the age of two or three. I have vivid recollections of an extreme dependence on others that I had outgrown even by the age of four. I remember, too, the sense of being so close to the ground that objects near the floor dominate my recollection, while I recall almost nothing of the tops of things. I recall clearly for instance, at the age of three, the pedals of a piano but much less the keyboard and what I now recognize to have been the cabriole legs of chairs and tables, but much less the tops. Not least, I recall the absence of distinctions such as I made a few years later. For example, my grandmother was very short, while one of my aunts was exceptionally tall, but I distinctly now see them in my mind as I saw them when I was two or three, when I was almost, if not quite, unaware of any difference in their size. Indeed, within some limits I could almost tell the age I was from the feeling tone of the experience as now recalled, although I have in fact objective means of determining it.

So much for a subjective test. Now let us look at possible objective ones. No kind of test, of course, could provide the type of proof one expects in a geometrical theorem; nevertheless, I think some of them can be very persuasive. One of the simplest is to return to a place one vividly remembers from an early age and has never since visited till, say, thirty or forty years later. I spent a brief vacation, for instance, at the age of two and a half at a cottage that

I never subsequently visited till about fifty years afterwards. The second visit was at about the same time of year, so the same sort of flowers and shrubs were to be seen. I could still smell the scent of some of them; but what a difference! Now it was hardly more than a vague whiff, while in my recollection of long ago it was as if the wallflower had wrapped itself round me and as if the roses had been shut up with me in the same bottle. All these years one of the most vivid recollections had been the sound of bees. I could still hear it on my return visit, but only a faint murmur. Perhaps but for the recollection of the early experience I could never have fully understood what Yeats meant by a 'bee-loud' glade.

There is, however, a much more interesting type of objective test: one in which one's reconstruction and interpretation of an experience as recollected proves to be less accurate than the recollection itself. I have two examples to offer.

The first relates to an experience I had on a day when I was four years and eight months old. The exact date is of public record, since it relates to the only occasion on which King George and Queen Mary visited the town where my parents lived at the time. I was taken to my grandmother's house because it commanded an excellent view of the procession. (My grandmother, by the way, was born in 1828 nine years before Queen Victoria ascended the Throne, and was very informative.) I was immensely interested in the outriders, because of their splendid uniform, and I remember making what may have been my first logical deduction: if they, who were merely attendants on the King, were so gorgeous, how much more resplendent must be the King and Queen? I expected both to be dressed as I had seen them in pictures and to be two storeys tall, which was the minimum height I had been accustomed to assign to God. To my immense disappointment, a drizzly rain ensued just as the royal carriage hove into sight. All I could see was the King taking off his silk hat in greeting; all except for one thing which throughout the years I remembered vividly: the inside of the cab seemed to be lined with purple. I could not see the Queen at all. For fifty years or more thereafter I maintained that I had seen the King in a purple-lined cab, which many people told me was unlikely. Only a few years ago I took the trouble to investigate. The local city librarian found me a newspaper account of the proceedings: the Queen had worn a petunia dress with matching hat and plume. My interpretation had been wrong; the recollection of my early childhood perception exactly right.

My second case relates to the cottage of the much earlier period when I was two and a half. How we reached the village I have never been able to recall; but I have always had a most vivid recollection of what happened when we got there. A pony and trap, the normal counterpart of a taxi in those days and circumstances, awaited us to take us to the cottage. I recall my wonderment in noticing that the radius of the two wheels was nearly my own height, so that the wheels alone stood almost twice my size. To get into the contraption, one used steps at the back. They were much too steep for me, so I was lifted up and (O joy!) permitted to sit with the driver, although with two adult hands restraining me from behind. What baffled me in later years was that the drive seemed in my recollection so short. For the shortness of the drive was difficult to square with the facts as I later wrongly determined them to have been. Everyone assured me that there were only two ways of getting to that village from our home. One was by paddle steamer, which would have landed us five miles from it; the other was by train, which would have brought us to within three and a half miles of it. So till comparatively recently I believed, in reconstructing my recollection, that the ride had only *seemed* short because of my happiness in it, for it is a commonplace that happiness makes time speed by. Only a few years ago I discovered that while there were indeed only two *normal* ways of making the journey, there was another way. During the summer months a special excursion boat plied the river, sometimes making a stop at the village whither we were bound. If, as now seems to me to have been the case, we had taken that third way, the ride would have been quite short: perhaps ten to fifteen minutes at a gentle clip. Once again, my recollection was better than my later interpretation.

My basic purpose in providing these examples from my personal store of recollections, along with proposals for their authentication, is to prepare the ground for assessing claims to recollections of previous lives and for trying to establish, if possible, what meaning might be attached to them. What I have done so far is, at most, to show that some claims of accurate recall of early childhood experiences may be more reliable than is often supposed. We may now go on to ask: if we take at all seriously claims to recollection of previous lives such as reincarnationists make, what *kind* of recollection might we expect it to be? Suppose, for instance, that you claimed to recall details of a previous life in the fourteenth century as, say, a Tibetan monk. Might I without unfairness ask you to recite for me, in the presence of a Tibetan scholar, some passages from the Tibetan Buddhist Scriptures such as a monk of that sort must have known? Surely not. Now that Latin has been largely abandoned in Roman Catholic liturgy, I find that some of my Jesuit friends who twenty-five years ago were able to recite Latin psalms almost as instinctively as they could eat breakfast are often unable, even after such a comparatively short time, to remember how to say a Latin grace. Nor would it be fair of you, if I claimed to have been a cab-driver in nineteenth-century Naples, to expect me to treat you to a volley of Neapolitan street language of the period. Nevertheless, I might well expect you to learn Tibetan more easily than most Westerners, and you might have good reason for suspicion if I simply could not show any natural ability at all in Italian.

Reincarnationists sometimes make very extravagant claims about their recollections of previous lives. While I certainly would not rule them out, I do find some of them very difficult to believe. I have nothing comparable to offer of my own in that line; but I do have some striking clues to possible recollections of previous lives, which I shall mention presently. First, however, let us ask what kind of claims to recollection might seem more credible than the sort I have suggested.

In *Random Harvest*, a between-the-wars English novel by James Hilton, the hero suffers traumas resulting in amnesia. Although he functions quite well in a way, he cannot remember his pre-amnesia life. The woman who loves him brings his memory back eventually. Although we are not told precisely to what extent it was recovered, we do learn on the last page or so that he had a flash of recognition and we are left in no doubt that love was the instrument that effected it. Generally speaking, should we expect any more of a memory that might be supposed to have been somehow carried over from a previous life? Surely not. After all, many Germans and others who have emigrated in early life to some part of the English-speaking world and lose all practical opportunity of using their native tongue virtually forget it after twenty years or more. No doubt they could relearn it much more easily than I ever learned German; nevertheless, they would have to relearn it. If that be true even without amnesia, how much could we expect of recollection of a previous life? Presumably a flicker of *déjà vu* or *déjà connu* is about as much as we could fairly ask for. A man might have been a senator in Rome under Caligula and be able to describe his equine colleague yet not know a Latin subjunctive without some teaching. Oddly enough we sometimes seem to get more than we could reasonably expect.

Although I cannot say I have any dramatic claims to clear recollections of a previous life, I do have something to offer that I do not think can be very easily explained apart from *some* such hypothesis. Nor could it be available to me but for early recollections such as those to which I have alluded and the nature of which I have described, for as we shall see they arise within that context. The fact that they pertain to such an early age is of some importance, because if my recollections are authentic at all, in the first place, they will not have been vitiated by the complex network of subsequent experience. That is why I have tried to establish their authenticity.

First let us look at a very early dream. I can confidently plot one as occurring a few months before my fourth birthday. It is probably the earliest dream that I can now clearly recall, although it is by no means the earliest of my recollections. Like most children, I dreamt often, and much of the content of my dreams till about the age of ten was commonplace: pursuit by lions and so forth. In this early dream, moreover, the basic imagery is easily accounted for. I clearly recall that while awake I had been trying very hard and not very successfully to read a story about a wolf and some children. (I had learned the alphabet from a chart my parents had provided when I was almost exactly three and a half years old and I clearly remember receiving on my fourth birthday a book of little poems and stories, which I could read passably well by that time. My precocity had been assisted by my grandmother's pre-Victorian principles of education: she insisted on my learning at least one new word a day, always accompanied by the spelling, which I thought was undetachable from the word; for example, 'ivy' was 'ivy-eye-vee-wye'. My literacy prospered accordingly.) At the end of the story was a line drawing which I can see today as though I were looking at the printed page. It depicted a wolf walking on his hind legs, with two children, one in each paw. He gave me the impression of being quite benign, even affectionate, at least for a wolf. Wolves were to me at that time a special symbol of hostility to humankind.

In the dream I found myself in the parish church at night, when it would be expected to be empty and securely locked. Parents and others were in my entourage. The church is a Scottish Presbyterian one and, although a medieval foundation, was furnished in Protestant fashion. To my horror, the principal door of the church suddenly opened and the wolf entered, walking upright like a man. Moreover, unlike his prototype in the picture book, he was dressed. Yet he was not dressed in a business suit which was at that time the only way I ever saw a man dressed. He was wearing what I can now describe as nothing other than a type of chasuble and alb, which I most certainly had never seen in my waking hours.[3] We were all afraid that he would turn round and see us, the consequences of which I assumed to be too frightful to contemplate. We decided on the strategy of hurrying quietly to the south transept, which was not far from where we were, hiding under the very high mahogany pews, and hoping the wolf would not see us. I recall a sense of having a clear advantage because of my diminutive size, while the adults had to bend and awkwardly contort themselves to accomplish the manoeuvre, which was definitely successful, for the wolf turned neither to the right nor to the left. As would befit a devout priest processing to the altar, he moved slowly with measured step and began to ascend steps which in fact *were not physically there*. When he had reached what was the nearest thing to an altar that Scottish Presbyterian tradition would have countenanced, he bowed. I saw all this, peeking above the pew. When he bowed I was so terrified that he would see me that I bobbed down out of sight. When curiosity forced me to peek again, he had turned round, facing straight down the nave with his arms extended as at the *Dominus vobiscum*. At this I abruptly awakened. I can still feel the sense of immense relief, for in the last moment of the dream I had imagined that his eyes were upon us and that in another instant he would pounce and devour us all.

One cannot appreciate the significance of all this without an understanding of my total ignorance at the time of anything pertaining to Catholic practice or ritual. It is absolutely impossible that, with my upbringing, I could ever by that time have seen a chasuble or an alb or the gestures of bowing or of turning as in the *Dominus vobiscum*. Not only was the whole performance alien to everything I could possibly have seen at the age of three; I never did see anything like it till I was about fourteen.

At that age I was developing an intense interest in Catholic doctrine, ritual, and practice. Shortly before then I had been still so ignorant of all that, and so bereft of anyone who would have instructed me, that when, in the Protestant privacy of my room, I tried to work out for myself how to do the sign of the cross, which by then I had read about, the ridiculous version I tentatively decided upon demanded an acrobatic skill not to be expected as a universal endowment among the faithful. When I did at last find some little prayer books and manuals (one of which, to my delight, did reveal how to make that ancient sign of Christian allegiance) I learned Catholic doctrine, practice and outlook with uncanny ease and mercurial speed. Everything in my upbringing even by that comparatively advanced age would have seemed against my doing so. My only advantage was a fairly sound basic training in Latin and much of that, even, had been in the context of excruciatingly dreary accounts of Caesar's military campaigns. My attitude to the Catholic world I then sought and discovered on my own was ambivalent; it included a considerable degree of suspicion and fear along with an overwhelming, irresistible attraction.

All this seems to me by no means explicable in merely psychological terms, as some might suppose. Be that as it may, obviously far more astounding is my nocturnal encounter with the wolfine celebrant, well before my fourth birthday, in the Protestant church I habitually attended on Sundays with my parents. It was all extremely vivid and still is, although at the time of course I could no more have interpreted the performance as now I must than could a European child be expected to appreciate Chinese opera.

Newman relates something slightly akin to my later develop-ments along these lines, although nothing such as the wolfine dream of my infancy. He tells that before he was fifteen he habitually crossed himself before going into the dark and that he had no idea how he could have come by such a practice, although he thinks he must have acquired the habit from 'some external source or other'. He goes on to relate that he had found, in an old school exercise book a device that 'almost took my breath away with surprise'. It showed his name, the date (11 February 1811), when he was approaching his tenth birthday, and the words 'Verse Book', for it was his first book of Latin verse. Between 'Verse' and 'Book' he had drawn a solid cross upright and next to it what might have been interpreted as a necklace but which he could not construe as anything other than a rosary with the customary little cross at the end of it. Again, he could not imagine how he could have seen anything of that kind so early in life, since in the Church of England of those days 'churches and prayer books were not decorated . . . as I believe they are now'.[4]

In contrast to later childhood, when I often longed to grow up quickly into the adult state I then envied, my attitude in early childhood was sharply different. Not only was I eminently content with my status as a child, at least up to the age of six; I clearly recall my sense of superiority. From occasional remarks people made I was reminded from time to time that before so very long I would grow up to be 'a big man'. That prediction, far from filling me with hope or pride, irritated me. As I recall my feelings in those early years, such promises came over to me as gloomy threats. Adults of all ages seemed to me to be, even the best of them, an inferior class. I did not dispute that I might expect to become an adult one day; but telling me so had the same sort of effect as telling a thirty-year old woman that before very long she will be old.

Moreover, I remember habitually feeling that I *had been* an adult and had *attained* my now vastly superior condition. Telling me I was to become grown up was therefore somewhat like telling a rich man who had been poor that one day he would be poor again. Adults looked so clumsy. I very clearly remember being lifted up by someone, seeing my baby face in the mirror, and feeling very pleased at the sight. I always assumed, however irrationally, that I had left an adult state behind me. I did not at all despise adults; I liked most of them very much and loved some of them deeply. But at the best they were somewhat like handsome horses: far stronger, but plainly not to be compared with anyone who had attained childhood. This feeling had nothing consciously to do, of course, with reincarnation. That would have been the last thing my parents or anyone else would have mentioned to me. It was just an assumption that I made and that remained with me till I was about six, then gradually disappeared.

I could recount innumerable other such stories suggesting a sense of my being no stranger to human existence, but I will conclude these examples with one incident that occurred when I was less (but probably not much less) than five. I overheard a conversation which, for all its casualness, confronted me with a reflection that was to me at that time distinctly novel. It was to the effect that but for my parents I should not have been here at all. I had not the slightest idea why that might be the case, nor did I care, but I took adult opinion seriously and this remark much troubled me. I was haunted by it. I kept trying to envisage the alternative, even to convince myself of any advantages it might offer, such as one's not having a cold in the head, which would presumably be impossible without a head. The whole concept of my non-existence, however, eventually baffled me. It was not merely that it filled me with unspeakable horror; it seemed to me contrary to what I took to be the facts of life. I felt that I had chosen my parents and with them the rest of my entourage and that if I had not done so then I should have chosen in some other way. Had I been sufficiently sophisticated I would have expressed myself by saying: 'One must exist; after all, one has been doing it for a very, very long time, and this is certainly no time to stop.'

All that I can hope to show from these examples (which surely cannot be entirely without parallel in other people) is that some of us do have experiences of a sense of previous existence that cannot be dismissed as easily as the usual *déjà vu* feelings of later life, most of which might be explicable in psychological terms. Perhaps some sorts of memory might be genetically transmitted; but the kind of recollection I have in mind seems to require an explanation such as a genetic one could not be expected to provide. It is true that genetic throw-backs might extend through enormous ranges of time and beyond known ancestry. The kind of awareness in question, however, is not like that of discovering, as many of us well might, that we have our grandfather's quick temper, our mother's industry or our great-grandmother's wantonness.

If it be anything important at all, it is, rather, awareness of having been in other circumstances, of having done other deeds, of having thought a different range of thoughts. It is awareness also of being a pilgrim, having 'no continuing city'.[5] It is not so much mere *déjà-vu* as a sudden jolt into the remembrance of another land, another age, before the deluge that death brought about, which had swept you through what Plato called Lethe, the waters of forgetfulness. First come little hints, little pointers, little clues. Many of us get no further. Such clues, however, may lead us on to a checking-out that in turn may modestly enhance the meagre content of these pointers. While I am still highly skeptical of very detailed descriptions such as some reincarnationists give of alleged lives in the past, I should be most reluctant to set aside altogether even the most extravagant claims. The temptation, especially in imaginative people, to fill in missing details is of course very great. But if, returning home in the middle of the night, you reported that you had just seen two lions walking across Lambeth Bridge and I found out later that there had been only one, I would commend you for your observation and alacrity in reporting rather than rebuke you for letting your fancy run riot.

Only by the instrumentality of a field of energy such as is symbolized in the old concept of the 'etheric double' or by some other ordinarily invisible storehouse of energy and memory power does it seem possible to make sense of the notion of recollecting past lives. Whatever be the entailments of such claims, however, Christians should entertain them with the utmost seriousness, since, as we saw at the beginning of this chapter, the Christian doctrine of the resurrection of the body presents us with the same kind of problem that must be faced by claimants to recollections of a previous life. In view of the centrality of the doctrine of resurrection, the Christian who cannot believe in the possibility of memory of a previous life must not only repudiate reincarnationism but abandon the Christian faith itself.

10 Reincarnation in European and American Literature Since the Renaissance

> I hold that when a person dies
> His soul returns again to earth;
> Arrayed in some new flesh-disguise,
> Another mother gives him birth.
> With sturdier limbs and brighter brain
> The old soul takes the roads again.
>
> John Masefield, *A Creed*

Western thought and literature since the Renaissance are not, of course, necessarily Christian. Apart even from the Jewish contribution, which has been immense, not least since the French Revolution and the influence of Moses Mendelssohn, many writers, statesmen, and others who have left records of their opinions and are even now uttering them cannot be said to be Christian in any specific sense. Nevertheless, so overwhelmingly influential has been Christianity as the dominant culture as well as the mainstream of religious thought that almost no one whose life has been spent mainly in Europe or America in the last two or three hundred years could have escaped the influence of Christian ideas or avoided participation at least to some extent in a Christian outlook. Before that time the question would hardly have arisen at all wherever Christianity had established itself. Even where it was late in doing so, as in the Scandinavian countries, its influence eventually became notable. Christian influence in the West has been so pervasive that the thought of even those most hostile to it (and in some cases to all religion) has been at the very least well tinged with a Christian dye. One can revolt against one's upbringing and even desert one's habitual environment; but one cannot entirely discard the influence of latter or forget that of the former.

The importance of that reflection for our purpose is plain. Since no one in the West, even on the fringe of Christian influence, can possibly escape that influence and is likely, on the contrary, to be immensely affected by it, emotionally, psychologically, intellectually, and morally, we cannot usefully make strong distinctions in Western literature between 'Christian' and 'non-Christian' writers in such a way as to permit us to say, when we find reincarnationist ideas in a particular writer, that he or she does not come within the general stream of Christian culture. Except for orthodox Jews and some others (and even then only to the extent that they have held themselves rigorously aloof from Christian society), no one can be accounted entirely outside the stream. My purpose in this chapter is to show that, contrary to a common belief, reincarnationist ideas are not at all alien to Western thought or peculiar only to India and civilizations influenced by her, but have prospered in the West, where they have had many distinguished exponents, whenever the special interests of the ecclesiastical hierarchy have not forced them underground. Since the Renaissance that sort of persecution has been generally somewhat less practicable, though it has by no means ceased.

We have already seen that the Renaissance humanists, influenced as they were by Platonic and Neoplatonic ideas, were generally hospitable to reincarnationism and sometimes, as in the case of Pico della Mirandola, exponents of it. So also, for similar reasons, were the seventeenth-century English Platonists. Henry More, for instance, whose thought and erudition both Coleridge and Samuel Johnson much admired, clearly taught reincarnationism. Dean Inge, much nearer our own time, says that no one could read the Cambridge Platonists 'without feeling that there was a real outpouring of the Spirit at Cambridge at this time, which in the future may engage more sympathetic attention than it has done yet.'[1] That is not to say of course, that all the Cambridge Platonists looked favourably on reincarnationism; but their literary interests opened their minds to it and, in an age in which the English clergy were often scandalously avaricious, lazy, and corrupt, serious discussion of such ideas did promote genuine spirituality and draw people's attention to neglected aspects of their heritage.

By this time numerous thinkers, artists, humanists, and poets, had appeared on the scene, each reflecting in his own way the spirit of the Renaissance. Many had expressed definite belief in transmigrationist ideas. Paracelsus and Giordano Bruno are well known in this connection, but the doors of ancient thought had been thrown wide open, so that transmigrationism was again in the air. We find traces of it in Spenser, who in the sixteenth century had written:

> A thousand thousand naked babes attend
> About him day and night, which do require
> That he with fleshly weeds would them attire:
> Such as him list, such as eternal fate
> Ordainéd hath, he clothes with sinful mire,
> And sendeth forth to live in mortal state,
> Till they again return back by the hinder gate.[2]

Shakespeare represents in his characters as wide a range of opinions and dispositions as have come from the pen of any dramatist in all literature; nevertheless, he does hint through many of them that some form of transmigrationism is to be taken seriously. In the most famous soliloquy of all Hamlet, as he contemplates suicide, ponders on what happens after death:

> To die, — to sleep; —
> To sleep! perchance to dream; ay, there's the rub;
> For in that sleep of death what dreams may come,
> When we have shuffled off this mortal coil,
> Must give us pause. . . .
> who would fardels bear,
> To grunt and sweat under a weary life,
> But that the dread of something after death, —
> The undiscover'd country from whose bourn
> No traveller returns, — puzzles the will,
> And makes us rather bear those ills we have
> Than fly to others that we know not of?[3]

John Donne, though he satirically denigrates those primitive forms of transmigrationism that envision the return of human beings into the bodies of animals, could write of

> This soul, to whom Luther and Mahomet were
> Prisons of flesh; this soul which oft did tear
> And mend the wracks of th' Empire, and late Rome,

> And lived when every great change did come,
> Had first in paradise a low, but fatal room.[4]

Even Milton toys with the notion:

> Or wert thou that just Maid who once before
> Forsook the hated earth, oh! tell me sooth,
> And camest again to visit us once more?[5]

Thomas Browne, in *Religio Medici*, also alludes to the concept of reincarnation with at least some interest.

Thomas Vaughan, whom Isaac Newton diligently read, wrote that the soul of man 'while she is in the body, is like a candle shut up in a dark lanthorn, or a fire that is almost stifled for want of air.' That is of course a very Platonic sort of notion and one that we might expect in a seventeenth-century writer interested in alchemy and the occultism of his day. We should hardly expect it, however, of his contemporary John Dryden, who, born into a Puritan family, became a Roman Catholic on the accession of James II in 1685. Yet in an ode to a lady he writes:

> If thy pre-existing soul
> Was form'd at first with myriads more,
> It did through all the mighty poets roll
> Who Greek or Latin laurels wore,
> And was that Sappho last, which once it was before.

The great seventeenth-century rationalist thinkers such as Spinoza and Leibniz, though they do not put transmigrationism into their systems, do occasionally hint at it, and not surprisingly, since their systems could be hospitable to such an idea.

In the eighteenth century the two great deities on the intellectual scene were Reason and Nature. Neither of these ideas is necessarily inhospitable to reincarnationism, so not unexpectedly we find it alluded to with considerable respect by many of that century's most eminent thinkers. Hume, for example, who denied the existence of the soul and laid the foundation for a form of skepticism that has been extremely influential in subsequent philosophical tradition, explicitly says in his essay on the immortality of the soul that if one does take the notion of immortality seriously, then 'The Metempsychosis is, therefore, the only system of this kind that philosophy can hearken to.' Voltaire even more pointedly applauded the reincarnationist hypothesis, remarking that, since resurrection runs all through nature, being born several times is no more remarkable than being born once; therefore the doctrine of metempsychosis is neither useless nor absurd. We have already noted in an earlier chapter Kant's speculations on transmigration from one planet to another: a notion that many today would not expect to find in any writer two hundred years ago and perhaps least of all in one of the greatest critical thinkers of all time. Kant's important German contemporary J.G. Herder, in his *Dialogues on Metempsychosis*, writes eloquently as a convinced reincarnationist, asking his readers to ponder whether a truly great man could have become what he is in one lifetime. 'I am not ashamed,' he writes,' of my half-brothers, the brutes; on the contrary, as far as they are concerned, I greatly advocate metempsychosis. I certainly believe that they will ascend to a higher grade of being, and I cannot understand how anybody can object to this hypothesis, which seems to have the analogy of all creation in its favour.' Another of Kant's contemporaries, Georg Lichtenberg, a mathematician and physicist, recounts that at the age of eight he was guided by an unusual boy of his acquaintance to the notion of transmigration and that he never could rid himself of the idea that he had died before he was born. Lessing also favoured the idea.

Goethe was a thoroughly convinced reincarnationist. 'I am certain,' he remarked at a friend's funeral, 'that I have been here as I am now a thousand times before, and I hope to return a thousand times.' His belief affected all his work. Benjamin Franklin at the age of twenty-two wrote an epitaph for himself, which has appeared in several versions. He expressed in it the notion that his body will be like the cover of an old book with its contents torn out and that the work will appear again in a revised edition. Fielding, in his novel *A Journey from This World to the Next*, tells of a person who, after death, meets many souls returning to life on earth. Both Blake (who was much influenced by Boehme and Swedenborg) and his friend Thomas Taylor were much interested in reincarnationist ideas. Jean Paul Richter, a very influential German novelist, wrote: 'The least valid objection to the theory of soul-circulation is that we forget these travels. Even during this life and without experience of a 'change of clothing', many conditions vanish from our memories. How then should we expect to recall the different bodies and the still more varied conditions we have experienced in previous lives?[6] Hegel, whose

influence on not only German but European and American
thought throughout the nineteenth century was to be, for good or
ill, incalculably great, easily accommodated aspects of reincarnationism within his grand system. In growth and change he saw the
emergence everywhere of new life. *Geist*, the supreme principle,
does not merely pass from one embodiment to another; it comes
forth from each embodiment in a purer and greater form. He
specifically recognised that metempsychosis as traditionally
understood exhibits this general principle in relation to individual
existence. This aspect of Hegel's thought has been often
overlooked; yet it is an entailment of his elaborate system.

One might object that Hegel and other thinkers and poets who
emerged in the Age of Reason borrowed their ideas on
reincarnation from Asian sources, so that, contrary to what I am
trying to show, it was, after all, an exotic import from India, not
indigenous to the West. It is true that Hegel and some others of his
age did associate reincarnationism with India and other Asiatic
cultures. We should recognize, however, that not only was their
acquaintance with Oriental thought and life very limited; their
understanding of it was confused. Even Hume and others, when
they talk of 'the Hindoos', show that they have very muddled
information about them and sometimes radically misunderstand
Indian attitudes. In the generalisations they make on the subject
they reveal the superficiality of their acquaintance. Their
ignorance was not at all culpable. Oriental studies, as they are
understood in academic circles today, virtually did not exist.
Although work in them had begun, it was still at an embryonic
stage and did not get under way till far into the nineteenth century. Europeans had in any case no need to go so far afield for a
reincarnationist outlook. It was already indigenous to Europe, well
established in the Platonic tradition and had for long bloomed
wherever special ecclesiastical interests had not extirpated it.

As we pass from the eighteenth to the nineteenth century and
the dawn of Romanticism, reincarnationist ideas burgeon pro-
fusely. They interested Shelley and Balzac, Victor Hugo and
George Sand. Wordsworth's well-known lines speak clearly:

> Our birth is but a sleep and a forgetting;
> The soul that rises with us, our life's Star,
> Hath had elsewhere its setting,
> And cometh from afar.

The American transcendentalists were full of the notion. To Frederic Hedge (who translated Herder), Emerson, Thoreau, and James Freeman Clarke, it is part of the general intellectual scenery. The fascination it exercises over so many American thinkers of this period is reflected in and matched by its incidence in American poets. Whitman and Whittier both allude to it with relish. Whitman's *Leaves of Grass* show definite adherence to reincarnationism. Poe, in *Berenice*, categorically affirms belief in reincarnation. In this short story, written in the first person, he describes the room in which his mother died and in which he was born and he goes on: 'But it is mere idleness to say that I had not lived before — that the soul has no previous existence.' He writes of 'a remembrance of aerial forms — of spiritual and meaning eyes — of sounds, musical yet sad; a remembrance which will not be excluded; a memory like a shadow — vague, variable, indefinite, unsteady; and like a shadow too, in the impossibility of my getting rid of it while the sunlight of my reason shall exist.'[7]

Echoes of the same preoccupation are found in Tennyson, in Ibsen, in Samuel Butler, in Flaubert, in Dostoievsky, in Herman Melville's *Moby Dick*, in Tolstoy, in Wagner, in Louisa May Alcott, in Gaugin, in Strindberg, and in many others. Dante Gabriel Rossetti wrote a reincarnational story. There can be no doubt that the evolutionary theories of Darwin and others that emerged in the nineteenth century, as well as the teachings of Annie Besant and other theosophists, had an enormous effect on the late Victorians. The novels of Marie Corelli, an immensely popular author in her day and Queen Victoria's favourite novelist, who was disparaged by literary critics for her less than felicitous style, were saturated with reincarnational themes. Among almost all classes in which ideas were discussed at all and in almost all countries that had inherited the tradition of Socratic humanism in its variegated guises, including the deeply christianised humanism of the Italian Renaissance, reincarnational notions were discussed. By the *fin de siècle* they had become, in many quarters, something of a vogue.

In our own century they have been widely expressed, being found, for example, not unexpectedly in Conan Doyle but also in Shaw and in Barrie, in Maeterlinck and in Joyce, in J. B. Priestley and in Aldous Huxley, in James Jones and in Henry Miller. Masefield[8] and Yeats were definitely on the side of the believers. George W. Russell ('AE') reorganized the Dublin Theosophical

Society and was much involved in reincarnational ideas.

Nor has the twentieth-century interest been confined to intellectuals and poets. Henry Ford explicitly reports that, dissatisfied with traditional Christian proposals about human destiny, he adopted reincarnationism when he was twenty-six years old. Two very different military men of our day, the American General Patton and the British Air Chief Marshal Lord Dowding, expressed firm belief in it. The latter, in a speech on vivisection, delivered in the House of Lords on 18 July 1957, also called attention to our ancestral affinity with the lower animals and to the neglect by Christian theologians of the implications of that affinity: a neglect to which I have referred in an earlier chapter of the present book. Lloyd George reported that when he was a boy the thought of heaven frightened him more than of hell, because he imagined it to be a kind of perpetual church service with God checking on attendance and seeing to the impossibility of even temporary escape. He eventually came to the opinion that we are reincarnated and that by that means we suffer for our cruelties and wrongs and reap the rewards of our kindlier deeds.[9]

One could go on almost interminably with examples. What I have tried to show in this chapter is merely the remarkable persistence and ubiquity of reincarnationist ideas in a traditionally and in some sense predominantly Christian society. My purpose here has been the modest but, I think, very necessary one of establishing that reincarnationism, which we saw much earlier in our study to have been in the background of the New Testament and patristic writers, has been by no means a forgotten concept in more recent times in Western society. It has been, indeed, very much in the minds of many of the greatest thinkers and other notable figures. Interest in it today has intensified. Thoughtful people today of every Christian tradition, whether they may feel repelled by it or (as do many) find it superlatively attractive, ought to face the challenge of its implicates.

Objections to it come from two quarters: philosophers and scientists on the one hand and, on the other, theologians and religious people. Some may be more impressed by the philosophical than by the theological objections; others may account the theological objections weightier. We shall consider the philosophical objections before going on to the theological ones.

11 Philosophical Objections and Reflections

> In the collection of facts, one cannot be over-cautious. But in the invention of theories, especially in a field so peculiar as ours, where analogies drawn from the existing sciences are almost useless, a canny and sober circumspection would be the greatest mistake.
>
> Professor H. H. Price, *Presidential Address,*
> *Society for Psychical Research, 1939*

This chapter will deal mainly with the mind-body problem that is at the heart of the most formidable types of philosophical and scientific objection to reincarnationism in its classic forms: the one that merits, I think, the most serious attention. We shall touch on some other points that may be helpful in unravelling the nature of the objection, even points that may have theological overtones. We shall exclude, however, for the present, all objections that are theological and religious rather than philosophical and scientific, deferring them till the next chapter.

We may usefully note at the outset that the very notion of survival after death seems a contradiction, not to say an absurdity. For 'to survive' means literally 'to live on', and to say that a person has died yet lives on seems to be logically of the same order as my saying that my house was demolished last night but, since I plan to rearrange things this morning, I invite you to dine with me this evening as usual. You might say: 'But your house cannot have been really demolished. Perhaps it has been badly shaken in an earthquake?' No, the Christian cannot say anything like that about death; he must insist that it is the reality that it appears to be. He must *also* insist that personal resurrection is a reality. The Christian, no less than his positivistic and materialistic acquaintances, insists on the finality of death, though he also says that by the power of Christ it is to be overcome. Yet if I could ever without absurdity say 'I died', I might go on without absurdity to say, 'I shall die and live again', because death would be an event that occurs more than once, so

123

that, however fearsome the reality of it, it is not unique in the individual's existence. That is, of course, what the reincarnationist does say. What we must clarify is the meaning of 'I'.

Resurrection is not in itself a particularly difficult concept; nor is reincarnation. On the contrary, forms of them both are commonplace in nature. We all learn as little children about the caterpillar, the chrysalis, and the butterfly. Recently I had to cut down to stumps almost flush with the ground two favourite bushes whose rich foliage had for more than twenty years performed a useful function but which were growing old and scrawny. Soon afterwards new shoots were rising around the old stumps and already the daughters are even lovelier than I had ever seen their mothers. My friends jocosely call it a resurrection, as indeed it is; but it is not the kind of resurrection to which the Christian looks forward. The new bushes have the same root system as the old, as genetically I have the same roots as my fourth cousin once removed; but the Christian's claim is not that at all. To say that I shall rise again in my great-grandchildren is certainly not a specifically Christian claim. The Christian says *I* shall rise again. Once again, who is this 'I'?

This question confronts us in some measure even in everyday life. Only one aspect of me is empirically visible. Otherwise I could never deceive you. Suppose you have to meet Harry Smith at the station. You have never seen him and have no particular interest in him. You ask a friend how you are to recognize him in the crowd. Your friend tells you he is six feet tall, slim, has a resolute gait, auburn hair and brown eyes with a cheerful glint in them. Your friend does not tell you he has a foul temper or that he is an exceptionally good father or that he is a Knight of the Bath, for such information would be useless to you, since you could not possibly see any of these qualities or accomplishments, unless he were wearing the ribbon of his Order, which would be most unlikely. If, however, you were asking a friend how you should vote, you might well know the candidates by sight; you would wish to learn, rather, about their character and experience, neither of which you could discern from mere physical appearance. Suppose, finally, that you were not voting someone into political office or the like but wanted to choose a confessor or spiritual guide, you would go much further. Even the second order of information would not content you; you would wish to know, so far as possible, whether he were endowed with those rare qualities you would seek in someone who was to nurture your soul. You might even say you wanted to see underneath all masks.

The ancient Indian thinkers posed such questions in their own way and in their own way provided a variety of answers. Typical was the assertion that there are layers of selves, each of which may be called 'I'. They thought of these layers, however, as detachable, as are the leaves of an artichoke. You could strip away the empirical self like apple peel and go on till you came to the core. According to one form of this model there are no fewer than seven selves. Beneath the 'gross' body is an 'astral' or 'subtle' one, invisible to ordinary eyesight but at least partly visible to those endowed by clairvoyance, which, let us note carefully, is not 'magic' but simply a finer kind of perception than is available by ocular processes such as enable me to see tables and smiles and frowns. Theoretically, at least, we could go on to the seventh, the inmost self: the one that is reincarnated. By this time, however, I must be supposed to have been stripped not only of the outward identifying features that can be listed on my passport but of all else: the personality you find so distinctive; my sexuality; my mental abilities and shortcomings; all that you and I recognize as 'me'. It seems, however, that I have not quite lost all, for I am still saying 'I'. But is it any longer the 'I' that I ever mean in any imaginable context? If a man wore a moustache I could easily identify him though he should shave it off. Even if his face were to be burned out of all recognition I might well recognize him by his voice. Even were he to undergo a lobotomy that dramatically changed his personality I might well find means of recognizing him. But if he were stripped of *all* that I associate with him, how could I identify him at all? more precisely, what would there be to identify?

For at least two reasons, this problem did not come across to the ancient thinkers in the same way that it confronts us. In the first place, they did not attach the same *kind* of importance to personal characteristics as do we. I easily enough appreciate the need to improve my health by fitness exercises, to prune my personality by discipline, and to enrich it by love. I cannot easily talk, however, as did many of them, as if I could strip off my body as one steps out of a swim suit or shave off my personality as a man shaves off a moustache. In the second place and even more importantly, the ancients could talk about the several layers as if they were all of the same universal 'stuff'; that is, it was not a question of different 'substances' or 'dimensions of being' such as 'mind' and 'matter' but of various finenesses of one 'stuff'. The question then might be raised: which is qualitatively superior? The materialists would say, as does Simmias in Plato's dialogue, that the coarser was the more important; but the contention of Socrates and the upanishadic teachers was that, on the contrary, it is the other way round, because the finer, they argued, *animates* the coarser, which is therefore dependent on it. Our scientific knowledge no less than our existential awareness rules out our resorting to either of these ways of thought.

If physics and biology have taught us anything at all about the history of our planet, they have shown us that, as life does not occur till organic matter has assumed certain complex forms, so mind does not emerge till organic matter has attained a still further degree of complexity, notably in brain and sense-organs. We never see organic matter separate from and independent of the inorganic matter on which it is based; that is, we never see life detached from that in which it lives. To imagine otherwise seems impossible except in the fantasy of Alice whose cat vanished yet left the smile. We must also observe, however, that the inorganic matter in which life is based has been transmogrified in becoming organic. What we call mind seems to be in the same case in respect of organic matter as is the latter in respect of inorganic matter; that is, mind depends on and is inconceivable apart from life, as is life apart from whatever it is based upon.

That this is so can be shown by considering the nature of a state of consciousness or complex of mental event. I say I am looking at the red cover of a book. Light-waves have impinged upon the retina of my eye, producing an inverted image of the perceived object. My optic nerve has been stimulated and the visual sensation has occurred. Up to this point the process is physical; it can be, at least theoretically, located in space. Yet as soon as my brain has dealt with the occurrence and the occurrence has been appropriated as my state of consciousness, it is no longer in space. By no means, even with the finest of instruments, could you detect it, for with instruments it would have to be in space, however minute the space, and spatially the consciousness is simply not anywhere; nor can it be. My toothache is not in my tooth; it is not even in my brain, though both tooth and brain are involved in it; nevertheless it is I who feel the toothache, not my tooth or even my brain. You can observe my contortions as I suffer and hear my groans; but in no way can you observe my state of consciousness. Only I can perceive my own state of consciousness. With extremely fine instruments you might even see what is going on in my brain when I have toothache or see red books or hear a composition by Sibelius; but in no way at all with any instrument could you have my experience of any of these stimuli.

From such reflections we can go on to propose (1) that states of consciousness are closely related to brain-processes, and (2) that they are nevertheless by no means to be identified with them.[1] To say with the old-fashioned materialist that my brain secretes thoughts as my liver secretes bile is to ignore the nature of a vast set of facts pertaining to my state of consciousness. The mental events that constitute my state of consciousness are at least as different from my brain-processes as are my brain-processes different from the tissues of my brain. Yet my state of consciousness could no more come into being without my brain-processes than could the latter occur without the very modest amount of brain tissue necessary for their functioning. Although my perception of red is not the same as the conditions that bring it about, these conditions (which include the capacity to see wave-lengths of light between 550 and 700 Amstrom units, which colour-blind people lack) must have existed before I can see red. They need not exist now. I might have lost my sight entirely and still be able to recall the experience of seeing red and, if more feebly, to enjoy it; but if the conditions had never been present I could not have, nor could ever have had, that particular state of consciousness.

The question then is: what is the relation between the mental and the physical? We have neither the space here nor, happily, the need to consider in detail the various answers traditionally proposed to this question. Many (e.g. those of epiphenomenalism, interactionism, parallelism) are plausible up to a point; none is entirely satisfactory. Nevertheless, I think we must say, at least, both that life is to inorganic matter and that mind is to life, as is solid geometery to plane. You can have two dimensions without a third; but you cannot have the third without the other two.

We now come to the still thornier (and for our purposes even more relevant) problem of personal identity. I continually keep referring to myself. Who precisely is the self to whom I refer? It often includes my body, as when I say, 'I shall come to dinner this evening as arranged'. You expect, then, of course, to see my body in the dining room. Sometimes, however, no reference to my body is necessary, as when I say that I think it would be unwise for you to seek to divorce your wife. In the act of making such a judgement it is not of the slightest consequence that I should have brown eyes or blue, be tall or short, or whether the university degree I have is in psychology or in architecture; I am perfectly entitled to make the judgement in any of these cases. If I were a woman, not a man, I might be accounted by some better qualified to make it and by others worse; but my entitlement to make it has nothing to do with any physical circumstance or condition.

My body, nevertheless, has several extremely important features differentiating it from all other bodies in the world, so far as I am concerned. I can watch your body move, touch it, and even compare its movements with my own; but mine is the only body I cannot get away from and the only body, moreover, that I can directly control. On the negative side, however, while I can see your body in various perspectives, I can see mine only in a mirror and never as well as I can see yours. My body seems, then, to be related to 'me' in the opposite way in which my mind is related to 'me', for, as we have noted, I am aware of my mental state but not of yours, except by doubtful inferences.

My relation to my body is, then, unique; but what of my relation to my mind? I might tell you 'I can move my arm', and if I were paralysed I might have to admit 'I cannot move my arm'. I can also say to you quite properly, however, that I have the grief of Mary Jones very much in my mind and I can equally well tell you that I have put out of my mind the idea of visiting China this year. It seems as though I stand apart from my mind as I stand apart from my body, although I cannot get away from either. What then is the relation between the mind that I control and the body that I also control? Only by a figurative and perhaps somewhat misleading usage can I say either that I have something *in* my mind or that my mind is *in* my body. Strictly speaking, my mind, being non-spatial cannot be *in* anything, nor can anything be *in* it. How can a non-spatial entity be related to a spatial one? Yet clearly it is : my thoughts are not my brain-processes, but my thinking cannot be performed without my brain-processes.

We now approach the fundamental question: who is the 'I' that not only lifts the arm but has the feelings and thinks the thoughts? To identify this 'I' with the sensations and the experiences themselves, as did Hume, will not do for a complete answer. It leads Hume himself into self-contradiction, as when he says, 'I can never catch myself'. To whom or to what does the 'I' refer? When I ask myself this question I can distinguish between myself, the experiencer, and the experiences that I have. Yet the 'I' remains somehow elusive. Is it on that account necessarily illusory? Surely not; but it remains none the less elusive.

Now let us ask instead: 'Under what conditions do I remain the same self as I was before?' I have grown a great deal since I was a baby. My growth has not been merely in height and weight; I have become an adult; my hair and my nails have been cut regularly; cavities in my teeth have been filled with gold; my appendix has been removed; every cell in my body has changed several times. Yet I have no doubt that I am the same *self*.[2] That I can properly call myself the same *person* that I was in the wolfine dream of my childhood, described in a previous chapter, is much more questionable. I neither look nor sound as I did then to those around me; nor, certainly, do I feel as I did then. Indeed, as reported earlier, I clearly remember striking differences in my self-awareness at the age of, say, two years, and at, say, five. I have neither the same thoughts nor the same feelings nor the same personality that I had even in my twenties. Who is the 'I' that professes to make such affirmations? Memory provides one obvious link; but if I had lost my memory as a result of shell shock in battle or in trauma consequent upon a car accident, you would recognise me as the same self that you knew before the misfortune occurred, even though I did not. So far as I am concerned, memory would be theoretically sufficient for the continuity that is sought for establishing identity with the little child I once was; but since I cannot have memory without a brain and cannot have a brain without a body and a nervous system of some kind, it seems I must have a body to provide the continuity. Moreover, since at death my brain dies with my body, does not that event make an end of the 'I' to which so many allusions have been made?

So, indeed, do many people suppose; that is, either they are unwilling to entertain the possibility of any kind of immortality or resurrection or other form of afterlife or else they specifically renounce belief in any such possibility. Those who, for good reasons or bad, insist on expectation of an afterlife are perfectly entitled to do so (all Christians included, of course, among them), but they must also expect to be called upon here and now to specify how they expect the continuity between the present life and the other one to be established. Although one has no right to demand that Christians provide full descriptive detail of their vision of the life of the world to come, one does have the right to ask for an intelligible statement of their hope. To provide one they must be able to give an account of how the indispensable continuity might be attained.

We saw almost at the beginning of our study that the statements Christians have traditionally offered on the subject have been at best unsatisfactory and at worst outrageously muddled. How can we improve upon them? What is most of all needed is a resolution of the problem of identity such as would provide a basis for continuity of the self from one life to another.

I am suggesting that the problem has been exacerbated by the traditional model in which my birth and my death are presented as once-for-all occurrences that are both to be for ever unique in my history. The problem of identity and continuity is difficult enough by any reckoning; but to provide for continuity between a fleeting life such as ours and one that is to endure interminably, with or without growth, makes the difficulty intolerable.

If Christians were to take the reincarnational hypothesis seriously, that aggravation of the difficulty, at least, would be eliminated. Birth and death would no longer have that curiously unique quality. The philosophical difficulty that would then remain would be largely that of preserving identity and continuity from one life to another across a chain or series of lives. Although both moral enhancement and biological development would be expected, they would be presumed to take place gradually, occasional special evolutionary 'leaps' notwithstanding. The principal problem then would be that of trying to connect the individual in this life with the individual in his or her preceding life and with his or her succeeding one.

As we have seen, it would not be necessary that memory be preserved intact across the boundaries of death and rebirth: even those of us with the best of memories forget much. It would be necessary, however, to preserve *some kind* of memory, at least something such as Bergson's 'habit-memory', and to provide for this when the individual moves, hypothetically, from one body to another we must have some 'bridge', either in the form of an energy-storage system or in the form of something such as the 'subtle' body that, according to ancient Indian speculation, accompanies our physical one and duplicates in its own way its most important activities. The former of these alternatives seems unpromising, since it creates yet another problem: that of carrying the mental furniture to the storage depository at death and carrying it back from it again at birth. We are left, therefore, with the other alternative, for which there is so far no empirical evidence (and probably never could be) such as would satisfy a positivist or materialist, but a remarkable and growing body of testimony from parapsychology and psychical research.

These are the lines on which a Christian can most usefully try to work out a theology of the life of the world to come. The type of philosophical objection made by Antony Flew and some others that nobody has ever seen such 'subtle' bodies or detected their effects on the physical universe seems to me trivial. Nobody has ever seen an electron and, although we believe we experience its effects and know something of the tremendous powers that lie within the nuclear structure, nobody in all human history, despite exposure to the same forces in the external world that affect us today, had recognized till the present century the existence of that invisible, submicroscopic world that has already revolutionized our understanding of physics. The 'subtle-body' hypothesis is, to say the least, by no means implausible and it could perform very well the needed function. There is no reason at all why bodies must always be so heavy or so obvious as are ours in order for them to provide for the functioning of life and of mind.

Biological evolution no longer presents educated people with any difficulty; but it is evolution of so-called species of life. What is distinctive about the hypothesis we have been considering is that it entails evolution of the individual. It does not necessarily entail the survival of *all* individuals, unless one posits the type of immortality theory characteristic of Plato and others in the ancient world, in which the 'soul' is indestructible. Not all individuals need survive. That is not part of the philosophical problem that confronts us, although it may be for some a theological one, which we shall consider in the next chapter. The philosophical problem, so far as it arises in the construction of an intelligible Christian eschatology, *is* the problem of identity and continuity. I think that a modern form of the ancient 'subtle-body' theory is by far the most promising and practical hypothesis.

12 Theological Objections and Reflections

> For he (Christ) has broken the power of death and brought life and immortality (*aphthasia*) to light through the Gospel.
>
> 2 Timothy 1.10 (NEB)

If we read the New Testament and other early Christian writers openmindedly and with such knowledge as we have of their cultural and intellectual background, we must admit that in what they say of life after death reincarnation may not have been in their minds at all. Nevertheless, we also find that what they say could be an admirable means of dramatising a reincarnational view in such a way as to prod their readers into action, which is every good preacher's goal: the moral and spiritual awakening of his hearers. From what we now know of the background of these writers some form of reincarnationism is not to be ruled out as a possible interpretation of Christian teaching about the life of the world to come. Much literary evidence has come to light in this century that encourages far more serious attention to this possibility. Although much more may be found in the future, it is unlikely that any such evidence could ever be so conclusive one way or the other as to compel a straight yes or no from everyone on that basis alone.

We have seen a variety of other reasons, however, why a form of reincarnationism need not be accounted incompatible with even the most orthodox understanding of Christian doctrine. Nevertheless, anyone of definite Christian conviction who feels disposed to accept any form of reincarnationism as an interpretation of the Christian hope or any aspect of it should consider what theological objections he or she must face. Since in the course of our study we have already considered the commoner ones, I shall merely state these here, develop the responses I make to them, and then proceed to a more serious and radical theological problem.

(1) *The moral (karmic) law, which is inseparable from all ethical*

132

forms of reincarnationism and is expressed in the general maxim that one reaps what one sows, takes no account of divine grace and therefore ignores, if it does not repudiate, the central message of the Gospel of Christ. The karmic law, though indeed inexorable, is no more so than is the essence of the Torah, which Jesus, according to the Evangelists, said he came to complete, not to destroy. Divine grace, divine providence, redemption through Christ: all these operate in, with, and through the law, not against it. There is as much room for love and grace in a reincarnational interpretation as in any other.

(2) *Reincarnationism encourages such an individualist approach to salvation that not only does it remove the need for the Church and for such ministry and sacraments as the Church deems necessary for salvation; it eliminates all need of guidance and help.* True, reincarnationism makes possible a 'lone walk' because it abolishes the need to depend absolutely on the Church's ministry and sacraments; but no reincarnationist, Christian or otherwise, would seek to dispense with whatever help is available. For Christians, the Church, as the unique instrument provided by God for our salvation, with all the sacramental structure and ministry it entails, is to be respected and loved, its follies and divisions notwithstanding. The fact that I can live alone does not mean that I wish to do so, much less that I disdain the company and the counsel of wise friends. Although it is possible for a bright person to learn mathematics by himself, how much better to have a good teacher. Many Christians recognise that they may look also for guidance from invisible helpers (saints and angels) and , as we have seen in a special chapter, reincarnationism stresses such a concept. Still, as Socrates pointed out long ago, no teacher can be more than a midwife; the student must do the work. Many great Christians (e.g. Kierkegaard, Tyrrell, Simone Weil) have found that the Church they have so deeply loved is not absolutely indispensable.

(3) *The expectation of a succession of lives and of the further chances they provide encourages procrastination.* True, but so also does even the span of life we have. Augustine's youthful prayer, 'Give me chastity but not yet', is as possible on one view as on the other. So long as the goal can be missed, the urgency is there. Yet the deathbed-repentance syndrome is familiar to all pastors and confessors.

(4) *The notion of paying the penalty for sins of a previous life that one has forgotten is immoral. One is not to be held responsible for what one cannot remember.* In fact, however, we generally forget how we acquired the bad habits we have and, as Christian theologians emphasize, we do not even know how distorted we are. The drunk driver has forgotten how he got drunk; but the accident he caused may kill his wife and blind his son for life. That our forgotten evil thoughts and deeds take their toll is both psychologically realistic and in full accord with the Christian doctrine of sin. The Christian doctrine of original sin can be indeed eminently well interpreted in reincarnational terms.

(5) *Reincarnationism is inconsistent with the Christian teaching that our destiny is settled once for all at death.* There is no such clear teaching; otherwise we could not talk as we do of cleansing or of growth. The notion of an unchanging condition of everlasting bliss or of everlasting torment is both contrary to everything the Bible tells us about the loving disposition of God toward his creatures and irreconcilable with what we know about the nature of the universe, including man.

(6) *Christian belief in the Second Coming of Christ and the* dies irae, *the Day of Judgment, is alien to a reincarnationist view.* It might be incompatible with some forms of reincarnationism but not all. Even if we understand the Day of Judgment literalistically as a culminating event in the history of man, we can still interpret it as the end of this age and the beginning of a new one: possibly (with the destruction of Earth) on another planet in our galaxy or some other. In any case, the holocaust that many Christians envision on that 'dreadful day' would presumably wipe out all life, including the vast animal kingdom to which we are biologically related. Christian theologians have never given serious attention to such matters, though we are assured in the Gospels that God notes even the fall of a sparrow to the ground.

Then again, are we to suppose that someone who has died an hour before the holocaust with a huge burden of guilt is to have his or her purgatorial sentence commuted while another has been suffering since the time of Cyprian, all on the principle of the parable of the labourers in the vineyard? If there be any moral development and any divine justice at all, surely opportunity is not to be wiped out suddenly, indiscriminately, and for ever, at the sound of Gabriel's trumpet? Models of this sort turn God into a monster, not only in his condemning some to everlasting punishment but perhaps even more in his denying opportunity to many. Adherents of such views seem to be worshipping the Devil rather than God, since only to the Devil could such cruelty be attributed; perhaps indeed not even to him. Origen and modern Universalists have seen this in their own ways. Much more compatible with God's love for all creation is a reincarnationist interpretation of the life of the world to come: one that includes, at any rate, a reincarnational programme, with the opportunities this affords for development and growth.

One may ask, as did the Cambridge moralist A.C.Ewing, in a sympathetic but critical reference to reincarnation, whether there may not be a 'mercantile flavour about the conception' of 'an exact proportion between such incommensurables as goodness and happiness', such as the karmic law envisions. He suggests that in a universe in which everything is so exactly arranged there could be no genuine self-sacrifice.[1] His point is well taken. Christian love knows nothing of such moral accountancy. Christ, far from calculating the cost of our redemption, pours forth his blood for us on the Cross. Is not the divine self-humbling of the Incarnation as understood in orthodox Christian teaching and especially as presented in the kenotic passage in Philippians[2] the supreme example of the outpouring of divine love with infinite abandon?

Yes indeed; but the cost of our redemption may be even greater then Ewing perceived. It would be greater than he represents it if, as Thomas Aquinas says, grace presupposes nature and perfects it[3] and as Jesus himself is reported to have said, the law is not destroyed but completed. For if God, in his self-humbling, must reckon with both law and nature, the cost of sacrificial love must surely be incalculably higher than we can conceive.

In any case, the problem of evil remains: the most intractable of all problems in Christian theology. It affects all living beings. As Professor John Hick notes towards the end of his treatment of it, in a useful passage on animal pain, the problem of pain may be even more perplexing in the case of lower forms of life than in our own case since with us it may serve a moral purpose, while in their case it can have no such role[4] according to traditional theological models. A reincarnational view, however, not only moderates that important aspect of the problem of evil by giving the lower animals a place, however modest, in the moral as well as in the biological scheme of evolution; it also much mitigates the problem in respect of human tragedy and injustice. It spreads the story of the individual on to a much larger canvas, so that in looking at our present life we are seeing only a slice (indeed a very slim slice) of what stretches far into the future as well as into the past.

Some Christians suspect that reincarnationism fosters the work-righteousness that the Reformation Fathers condemned in the late medieval Church. I am inclined to fear a lazyminded and immoral antinomianism in the Church much more than any excessively moralistic tendencies. The work ethic, for all its limitations, has played an important part in the history of the Christian Church, for example in the great tradition of Benedictine monasticism (*orare est laborare*: to pray is to work, to work is to pray) and in the very different tradition of the English and American Puritans. In any case, however, a reincarnationist view does not in itself engender reliance on either faith or works. In India, two schools, *bhakti-yoga* and *karma-yoga*, whose respective emphases correspond very roughly to these, are equally reincarnationist. No doubt if a form of reincarnationism found general acceptance in the Christian Church it would not make any notable difference at all in that matter.

What, according to the mainstream of orthodox Christian teaching, does Christ do for us? What is the nature of his redemptive work? However the various theological traditions express it, it is always seen as a provision of the conditions that make possible my salvation. Through faith in him I am justified, that is, I am 'put in the right way', so that it is now possible for me, as it was not before, to get myself out of the mess I was in and be 'sanctified'. We might express that by saying that whereas I had got into such a bind that, practically speaking, my moral evolution had come to a halt and further progress was impossible, Christ has come to my aid in such a way that by appropriating his spiritual power I can make progress once again. It is that discovery that causes me to be, in C. S. Lewis's phrase, 'surprised by joy'. Reincarnationism does not in the least injure this vital aspect of Christian teaching; it illuminates it by putting it into more intelligible terms.

Much more theologically serious is the question of Jesus Christ's own position in the evolutionary scheme that all ethical forms of reincarnationism presuppose. According to Chalcedonian orthodoxy, he is 'True God and True Man.' As God he stands outside the reincarnational scheme, being himself its principle, its source, and its goal; but as man he must be within it. One must not cavalierly resort to the argument that he may be a special case, since the official teaching of the Christian Church, on both sides of the East-West schism and on both sides of the Reformation curtain, is that, although sinless, he fully shares our human condition. Of course by no means all who profess Christianity adhere to Chalcedon; but the problem is nevertheless present, if in a different form, for these others too. For Jesus, even to the most heterodox Christian, must stand in a very special place in human history, to say the least. The problem in its most acute form, however, arises in terms of Chalcedonian orthodoxy, and it is in that context, therefore, that we should primarily consider it.

The Christian claim, as expressed in ancient formulae such as the Nicene-Constantinopolitan and the Chalcedonian creeds that emerged in the fourth and fifth century respectively, is that Jesus Christ has by any reckoning a unique status. Although he shares in the fullest way in the human condition, his status is different from that of every other human being. He introduced a new age, an age that will in turn give place to a new one again at the Second Coming. No one in the fourth and fifth centuries knew anything of the magnitude of the universe of suns and planets scattered in unimaginable distances across incalculable numbers of galaxies; they knew little, indeed, of our own planet Earth. It would be, on the one hand, difficult, not to say artificial, to interpret them as having meant that Jesus Christ is Lord of the cosmos: a cosmos of which they had no inkling of an idea. To say that they so intended would mean, for example, that if there are (as surely there must be) intelligent beings on other planets either in our own or in another galaxy, then as soon as we establish communication with the inhabitants of such a planet we ought to determine at once whether they know that their Saviour and Lord came to *our* planet to save *them* and, if they do not know this, we ought to collect money to send missionaries to them or at least conduct an evangelical campaign by means of radio signals. On the other hand, to argue that, since the world known to the ancients who formulated these creeds excluded not only the Americas and large areas of Asia and Africa but even considerable sections of Europe, we should confine the Lordship of Christ to those areas they could have known would surely be artificial, not to say absurd.

Long before anyone knew of the outer galaxies or could have needed to face, as do we, interplanetary communication and travel as practical possibilities, Alice Meynell (1847-1922), in one of her most remarkable poems, hinted at the problem that the magnitude of the universe poses for Christology. Entitled *Christ in the Universe*, it contains these allusions:

> No planet knows that this
> Our wayside planet, carrying land and wave,
> Love and life multiplied, and pain and bliss,
> Bears, as chief treasure, one forsaken grave.

> Nor, in our little day,
> May His devices with the heavens be guessed;
> His pilgrimage to thread the Milky Way,
> Or His bestowals there be manifest.

> But in the eternities,
> Doubtless we shall compare together, hear
> A million alien Gospels, in what guise
> He trod the Pleiades, the Lyre, the Bear.

> O be prepared, my soul!
> To read the inconceivable, to scan
> The myriad forms of God those stars unroll
> When, in our turn, we show to them a Man.[5]

Although we are left in a quandary about what it means to say that 'Jesus Christ is Lord', I think we must put *some* limitations in respect both of place and of time. This is in no way to limit his role 'for us men and for our salvation'. So far as we Christians are concerned there is 'no other Name', no other Saviour to do for us what he has done and does. We can then go on to see Jesus as the unique embodiment, the full and final revelation of God to humanity on this earth and for this age, the age that is to end and give place to a new one at a presently indeterminable date.

The question then arises: is Jesus himself within the evolutionary process that is inseparable from reincarnationist teaching? To this question we may give the answer that he is at the end of it, so far as this age, this aeon, is concerned. He has gone beyond us. He, the Risen and Ascended Christ, reigns, as Christian devotion puts it, with God. To pretend to be able to speculate on what precisely is his work or his function in the new dimension whither he has gone or in the new age that his Second Coming will herald would be arrogant and futile. All one may dare to say on so awesome a topic is that surely there must be higher and higher reaches of development and growth such as are in the nature of the case far beyond our present imagining. We might perhaps, if timidly, speculate on what may lie in store *for us* in a future age of evolutionary development; but we certainly dare not speculate on his role except in so far as we have the assurance of his protection for ever and the knowledge that through him salvation is available to us. That is all we need to know, as Christians, about our Redeemer, whether in orthodox, traditional fashion we acknowledge him to be 'Very God and Very Man' or in a more heterodox vein account him *filius adoptivus*: the adopted Son of God. I happen to be among those who think the first of these two formulations is, despite the great interpretative difficulties, the less misleading, so I range myself on this point with the traditionalists. I would note, however, that if I, with my orthodox stance on the nature of the Incarnation, can argue as I have argued here, those of more heterodox opinions should find it even easier to do so.

In conclusion we naturally ask: what is the purpose of this unthinkably elaborate evolutionary process? Questions of this kind arise for all educated people today, irrespective of reincarnationism. Why should not God create with the wand-waving that has been traditionally attributed to him in interpreting Genesis? I have discussed this complex question elsewhere.[6] Here I would simply point out that the creation of anything so morally valuable as man takes billions of years and enormous effort on the part of the evolving creature. Further development must inevitably take more still. Since it will be attended by greater and greater dangers our need for the work of Christ and for the aid of all the invisible helpers we can get will become more and more urgent as we ascend the evolutionary spiral. Self-discipline is only one of the instruments we must perfect; the power of love, the acquisition of which entails far nobler and more poignant self-sacrifice, will be even more necessary.

What then is the goal? Or indeed may we speak of one at all? Not so very long ago, in evolutionary terms, the goal was to stand upright, to speak, to conceptualize. Now all that is far behind us. With the development of individuality our next goal must be very different. Is there a final goal? Or is there, rather, a fundamental principle drawing us, or some of us, nearer and nearer the ambit of God, apprehending him more and more intensely, serving him more and more joyously, and appropriating ever increasingly our capacity for the Beatific Vision? To questions of this kind we shall be attending in the next, our concluding chapter.

13 The Life of the World to Come

> Then the One sitting on the throne spoke: 'Now I am making the whole of creation new,' he said.
>
> Revelation 21.5 (JB)

> There are many rooms in my Father's house;
> if there were not, I should have told you.
>
> John 14.2 (JB)

In the continuing process that we must now see as a corollary of all that we know about our evolutionary past, how is our salvation through Christ to be worked out? Although plainly we cannot know the details of the geography of the world to come, we may surely ask with propriety, if not also as a matter of moral and intellectual duty: how ought we to delineate the Christian hope we profess? What, in general terms, is our vision of 'the life of the world to come'?

In the chapter on purgatory I have suggested that the intermediate state commonly called purgatory is more intelligibly interpreted in reincarnational terms. That means, as I suggested there, that we are already in that state; that is, purgatory is a continuous process. We have been embodied before and we shall be embodied again, till the gold is all sifted out from the dross. We have learned much; we have still much to learn. The learning is at once painful and joyous.

Within this general framework, each person will have his or her own vision of 'the life of the world to come'. for each will see everything from his or her own particular stance. I can offer only my own, in hope that it may help those who are in general agreement with me to construct theirs.

I expect when I die to discard my present flesh-and-bones body and accustom myself to the nakedness of the body of light that has been all along its concomitant and (except to the clairvoyant) invisible counterpart. I certainly expect to be confronted by the

141

Lord Jesus Christ as soon as I am capable of it and to receive from
him an assessment of my progress in the life I have just completed,
together with an account of my future needs. This part of my vision
corresponds to what is traditionally called 'the Particular
Judgment'. I look forward to this confrontation with loving awe. I
do not fear the encounter. My fearlessness is certainly not due to
any pretensions to perfection. It arises, rather, from a deep faith in
Christ and confidence that he will both encourage me by
approving what I have done well and also show me what I must
still do, especially in the next embodiment. I do not expect that he
will choose that embodiment for me, for that would be to handicap
if not to enslave me in such a way as to thwart my advancement by
hampering my capacity to make the best use of my circumstances.
I hope, therefore, that he will guide me where I can most
profitably look for and then choose my next embodiment, either
on this planet or on another, and which type of parents and other
circumstances might best promote my growth. I expect to have the
assurance of continuing awareness of his blessed presence and of
his aid. I expect to be confronted by the temptation to luxuriate in
his love when I ought to be responding to it by further adventures
under his banner.

My primary task will be finding the next embodiment. It may
take a long or a short time; it may be easy or difficult. That will
depend on a variety of conditions such as the acuteness of my
spiritual vision and my moral readiness to accept possibly
unpleasant conditions. Yet my duties while in the subtle body
may also include, for instance, finding opportunity to help friends
on earth. I certainly expect to be much helped by even the least of
their prayers for me, for I see the traffic as two-way. I expect to
suffer intense longing for further embodiment, for I shall see with
increasing clarity how necessary that is for my advancement and
how marvellous the opportunity it will afford. I expect to be
confronted by many choices, some of which are likely to be very
difficult ones, until at last I do make the decision and throw myself
into it. Much will depend on the quality of the decision. I expect to
be often frustrated in my quest till at last the right opportunity
presents itself and the embodiment is available.

I have alluded to the quality of the decision on which so much is
to depend. What precisely does this mean? What, for example,
would constitute an inferior decision? In what ways would it hinder
me?

Suppose I were to make a choice that gave me the opportunity of indulging futile fantasies I might have entertained in my present life. That would certainly hinder my progress, exacerbating the 'bad karma' I had already accumulated. One might be so eager to taste once again the joys of carnality as to leap at the first opportunity without regard for what the embodiment might do for one's moral and spiritual advancement. At a much higher level, one might have great difficulty in choosing between two possibilities, each eminently good in itself, each valuable for one's spiritual evolution. Especially crucial might be a choice that entailed accepting or rejecting the opportunity to make a major 'leap' such as occasionally arises in evolutionary processes. Ought I to take the opportunity now? Am I ready for it? Or ought I to postpone such a move to a later occasion: one that might not arise for many embodiments to come?

In light of such considerations we may be able to see more clearly the precise force of the traditional prayers for the dead. *Requiescant in pace, et lux perpetua luceat eis*: may they rest in peace, and may light perpetual shine upon them. In the state between embodiments (as in a state of fervent prayer) what is needed above all else is quietude, peace, in preparation for the great decision that must eventually be made. For the quietude to be profitable, however, it must be enlightened, illumined by the clarity of the light of Christ. Finally, since at the end of a life on earth, with all its struggles and trials, the most valiant of pilgrims is likely to be tired out, the brilliance of the light cannot be adequately appropriated until the fatigue has been removed. So we need refreshment, light, and peace, which is precisely what is besought in the traditional 'Commemoration for the Departed' in the Roman Mass: *locum refrigerii, lucis, et pacis.*

To ask how many deaths and re-embodiments await me seems to me somewhat like asking when the world is coming to an end. How could I know? Nor can I possibly say in how many other planets I may have to pitch my tent, having the opportunity of finding the right embodiment for this or that particular stage of my pilgrimage. Perhaps, though it seems to me unlikely, I shall have completed, on my death, the last of my embodiments on this planet and must seek elsewhere. Perhaps, though it seems to me unlikelier still, I shall have reached the end of the present age and shall be plunged into a new one. That would be presumably what is traditionally called 'the General Judgment', in which I should see a crucial reckoning. Confident that my Saviour has my name in the Book of Life, but by no means confident of the extent of my appropriation of it, I do not expect to be called upon to sit back in everlasting enjoyment of heaven, whatever that could mean.

When, eventually, I do pass into that new age that is promised, I cannot expect that I shall be in a state such as could be called 'eternal'. Only to God can eternality be ascribed. I do hope, however, to be able *to participate* more fully in the eternal bliss of God, and to go on and on with further embodiments that can make that participation more and more realizable. These further embodiments may be more and more rarefied in nature; but whatever they are they will always be adapted to my evolutionary needs.

There may be stages in the process beyond the mode of consciousness we call 'individual' (inconceivable to me now), but if so then I must suppose that they will somehow subsume individuality at its highest intensity as an element in whatever may lie beyond it. Whatever lies beyond it could not erase individuality, the highest mode of consciousness we now know: one whose peculiar value God will not discard.

The vision I am presenting is specifically Christian in its preservation of individual awareness of myself in my relation to other selves and above all in my relation to God. I do not see myself as ever losing that awareness; I expect, rather, its intensification, though also, no doubt, its enhancement by other dimensions of consciousness. Nor can I see anything static in any future that could possibly be in store for one who, like myself, has been created by God through an evolutionary process and redeemed by God's acting in the evolutionary process through the human embodiment of Jesus Christ for me and my salvation. There is nothing static in the promise held out by Deutero-Isaiah:

> Young men may grow weary and faint,
> even in their prime they may stumble and fall;
> but those who look to the Lord will win new strength,
> they will grow wings like eagles;
> they will run and not be weary,
> they will march on and never grow faint.[1]

Then is the process never to end? Is the evolutionary spiral to go on for ever? Certainly there can be no 'deification'. That is definitely and fundamentally excluded by our Christian stance. What, then, if one should ask: 'But what of heaven?' Or, more pointedly: 'To what is the intermediate state intermediate?' To answer such questions I think we might usefully glance at the way in which heaven has been presented in the great medieval Catholic tradition, within which Thomas suggests that it is essentially the apprehension of God. This is the Beatific Vision. The act is fully voluntary; it is an act of the will; but the essence of the vision is cognitive, that is, intellectual in the Aristotelian sense of contemplation. To know God as the blessed know him *is* heaven. There can be no higher beatitude for human beings or for angels. The blessed in heaven do everything easily, without fatigue. *In this respect* they are like the gods of ancient Greek imagining. Their efficiency springs from their being attuned to the divine energy. At all times they are apprehending energy at its source, which is God himself. They are perfectly happy (*makarioi, beati*) because they are as completely full of the divine energy as they can be. Thomas, asked how a great saint and a miserable little sinner who merely scraped into heaven could both be said to be perfectly happy, replied in effect that they are like cups, one a very large, the other a very small one, but both cups perfectly full. This is a beautiful vision of heaven, except that the little cup must remain little for ever and even the large one has had its size permanently set.

If, however, we translate this vision of human destiny into reincarnational terms, we can begin to see in it a greater dimension. Must heaven be so completely set and unchangeable? Must there be no advancement in it? To people at level one, level two is heaven; to people at level two, so is level three. When I move from one state of consciousness into another that is more advanced and therefore more complex, my experience changes in two ways. First, I suffer more, for I have to work harder than ever before. That is the purgatorial concomitant and consequence of my advancement. But then, second, I enjoy more, having achieved a new capacity for a new dimension of enjoyment. That is the heavenly concomitant and consequence of my advancement. In short, if we must use the traditional terms, we are translated to purgatory and heaven at the same time.

Then heaven does 'go on for ever' and there is also no end to the levels of advancement? Surely yes. To say otherwise would entail either (1) that I, a finite creature, can eventually reach an apprehension of God so perfect that I could find nothing more to

discern in the infinite glory of God and therefore had reached
the end of the road (a dismal prospect to anyone who appreciates
the glory of God) with nowhere else to go 'for all eternity' or else (2)
that God for ever restricts me to the capacity I happen to have
when I die. Both alternatives seem to me puerile. Why should not I
go on interminably, improving my capacity through discipline and
service and also enjoying the fruits of that capacity with every step
of my advancement?

Heaven and purgatory, then, on the view I am proposing, are
both elements in 'the life of the world to come'. The notion that
both are interminable does not in the least diminish the joy of
heaven. The pianist who practises six hours a day to perform once
in the evening does not enjoy his performance less because he is
concomitantly disciplined by practice.

Hell, as a state of 'everlasting punishment', that is of torture,
mental or physical, seems to me and to many others an odious, not
to say barbarous, notion. As traditionally depicted (even in the
highly intellectualised form in which it is presented by Thomas
Aquinas as *poena damni*, the pain of the loss of God) it would be a
futile waste of cosmic energy. The notion, however, that many
people might be simply extinguished, fading gradually out of
existence, seems to me more intelligible. Such people do not want
existence. Why, then, should the gift be thrust upon them? Others
will endure anything rather than lose the priceless gift. These will
go on evolving.

Henry Drummond pointed out long ago that when the concept
of biological evolution came home to the world at large, people at
first thought of it as having taken place in the past, as if it had no
future. Drummond saw all human history, past and future, as a
continuing evolutionary spiral. As in the past many fell by the
wayside, so in the future many will fade out of the picture.
Drummond saw the whole concept of the Kingdom of God in
evolutionary terms.[2] I account this a peculiarly important insight
upon which to construct a Christian eschatology. No vision of
heaven that excludes growth can ever do justice either to the
infinite greatness of God, the riches of whose Being are
inexhaustible, or to the concept of happiness itself as it could ever
apply to the experience of a finite being.

Here, then, lies the inevitable parting between an eschatology
for the Christian Way, to which I adhere, and proposals such as
other religions may care to entertain. The vision I am proposing

stands or falls as a *Christian* vision of the life of the world to come. Were it merely a championing of reincarnationism *per se* or yet another flight of fancy within the endless gnosiologies in which the major religions of the world freely abound, then this entire book of mine would have been indeed an exercise in futility. We Christians must be no less wary of false gnosiologies than were those who heeded Paul.

Buddhism, for example, attracts many Westerners, who find in it aspects of truth that are too often neglected in Christianity, especially in certain of its traditions. Buddhism has a very special history. For all the multifaceted forms in which it appears, whether dubbed Hinayana or acclaimed Mahayana, whether Therevada or Japanese Zen, whether Tibetan or Chinese, it remains historically an outgrowth whose original roots were in the sub-continent of India, where it no longer exercises any notable influence in any of its manifestations, while its Hindu parent continues to flourish mightily in many forms. Through the highly elaborate structures of Buddhist thought (especially Mahayana) there has emerged an interminable dialogue involving a seemingly endless flow of discussion with a cornucopia of distinctions designed to nurture it. Such discussions remind an educated Westerner of those that plagued the West in fourteenth- and fifteenth-century scholasticism, when the creativity of the golden thirteenth century had fallen into decline. Buddhists seem to have been able, for one reason or another, to play the game longer with not so much as a flick of Occam's salutary razor. (Perhaps Walter Lowrie who, in mischievous moods used to call Roman Catholicism Mahayana Christianity, may have had something of this in mind.) But both Buddhism and Christianity, when they emigrate to distant lands and are transplanted to very foreign soils are peculiarly susceptible to the danger. Christianity has been plagued by false gnosiologies from the days of Paul down to the present, and Buddhism has produced a no less luxuriant crop of unhealthy foliage and unprofitable fungi. Christian students of the religions of the world cannot be too wary of falling prey to the enticement of such traps, whether within our own fold or beyond it.

Wise, then, is our Lord's counsel: 'by their fruits ye shall know them'.[3] I am immensely sympathetic to those of my fellow Christians who suspect reincarnationism as one of the extraneous weeds that has no place in the ongoing life of the Church. Nevertheless, for the reasons given in the course of this book, I believe their fears on this particular score to be entirely unwarranted. Dangers, however, do abound; not all forms of reincarnationism are compatible with an authentic Christian hope. That is why I stress so much the necessity of seeing in what form reincarnationism can properly be christened.

Christians, in cherishing so much the values of the individual, thereby cherish no less the significance of personal relationships. Christian friendship, as the bearer of the *agapē* of Christ himself, is inseparable from Christian life. Such a relationship cuts right into the heart of individual consciousness. The intimate personal love that flows to and from our friends leaves an indelible mark on a Christian's inmost being. Symbolized in the Church's doctrine that a priest is a priest for ever, bearing always in his soul the indelible mark of his priesting, it is a fact of Christian experience that all specifically Christian relationships are a special kind of reality. The relationship does not merely mark our souls; it permeates our whole being like a fast dye. If individuality is to be in any way preserved after death, as of course reincarnationism plainly implies, so also must be preserved with it the relationships that have attended the expression of it in Christ.

Of Christian marriage all this is pre-eminently the case. Christian marriages, being indeed 'made in heaven', are not by any conceivable stretch of any Christian imagination dissoluble on earth. That, too, is symbolised in the Christian attitude to divorce. Few marriages, alas, are so authentic, even among those blessed by the Church. That is why it is not divorce that should be made difficult but marriage. In the life of the world to come I should certainly not expect to retrieve my wife and take up marriage again as if we had been on a long vacation apart and had returned home. Nevertheless, vastly changed though we might be (and as I should expect us to be), the notion that we could have preserved our individuality yet not seek one another out is unthinkable. No Christian man or woman, therefore, who sees the Christian hope in reincarnationist terms need doubt for a moment that such relationships can ever be lost: transmuted, yes; lost never. If they could be lost, so also would have been the individuals in whom the relationships had been begun and who had consecrated them for ever. This does not mean that 'soul-mates' are to be remarried with each re-embodiment; it does mean that the relationship, having become part of the individuals concerned, will always affect them wherever they go in the life of the world to come. The absence of the other party to the relationship will always be attended with a longing. When the longing is fulfilled, the fulfilment is attended by a peculiar kind of joy entirely unlike that of meeting anyone for the first time.

I have written this book to show that as Christians we can find in the reincarnational hypothesis an infinitely better understanding of the ways of God to man and of the love of Christ for the people he has redeemed. We must be cautious in what we do with such new insight as we may have achieved. In our excitement over the plausibility of a principle let us carefully avoid all foolish claims to know the details of the future pilgrimage. Who dare measure the mercies of God? Above all, let us anchor our vision in Scripture, which alone can provide a fitting conclusion to such a book as this:

> But still we have a wisdom to offer those who have reached maturity: not a philosophy of our age, it is true, still less of the masters of our age, which are coming to their end. The hidden wisdom of God which we teach in our mysteries is the wisdom that God predestined to be for our glory before the ages began. It is a wisdom that none of the masters of this age have ever known, or they would not have crucified the Lord of Glory; we teach what scripture calls: *the things that no eye has seen and no ear has heard, things beyond the mind of man, all that God has prepared for those who love him.*[4]

Notes

CHAPTER 1: THE NATURE AND IMPORTANCE OF THE QUESTION

1. 1 John 5.7.
2. 1 Corinthians 15.35—42 (NEB).

CHAPTER 2: CONFUSION IN TRADITIONAL CHRISTIAN OPTIONS ABOUT 'THE LIFE OF
THE WORLD TO COME'

1. Ezekiel 9.10.
2. Psalm 6.6.
3. Psalm 139.8 (JB); cf. Deuteronomy 32.22, Amos 9.2, Isaiah 7.11.
4. Acts 23.8.
5. 2 Corinthians 12.2
6. 1 Enoch 48.9. Enoch, among apocryphal books, was very popular with early Christians.
7. It is so used in this general sense in Nehemiah 2.8, Song of Solomon 4.13, Ecclesiastes 2.5.
8. Luke 23.43.
9. Daniel 12.2
10. E.g. 2 Maccabees 7.9, 14.46.
11. Matthew 22.23, Mark 12.18, Luke 20.27, Acts 23.8.
12. 2 Timothy 2.17.
13. Romans 6.23.
14. 2 Timothy 2.18.
15. Oscar Cullmann, 'Immortality of the Soul or Resurrection of the Dead,' in Krister Stendahl(ed.), *Immortality and Resurrection*(New York: Macmillan, 1965) p.45. Cf. Acts 17.32.
16. Mark 10.17.
17. Philippians 1.23.
18. Gregory of Nyssa, *De anima et resurrectione*, in Migne, *P.G.* 46, 108D.
19. Tatian, *Oratio ad Graecos*, 6.
20. Revelation 20.4 ff.
21. Justin, *Dialogue with Trypho*, 5.
22. Ibid. 80.

CHAPTER 3: WAYS OF UNDERSTANDING THE CONCEPT OF REINCARNATION

1. Act iv, Scene 1.
2. Psalm 19.7.
3. Psalm 89.1.
4. Thomas Aquinas, *Summa Theologiae*, I, 2, 2 ad 1.

5. Matthew 5.17.
6. E.g. the Parable of the Sower, Mark 4.3—20, 2 Corinthians 9.6, Psalm 126.5—6.
7. Lynn A. de Silva, *The Problem of the Self in Buddhism and Christianity* (Colombo, Sri Lanka: The Study Centre for Religion and Society, 1975) p.112.
8. Hebrews 13.14.
9. Mark 8.36—37 (NEB)
10. Matthew 27.50 (KJV)
11. G. F. Moore, *Metempsychosis* (Cambridge, Mass: Harvard University Press, 1914) p.56.
12. H.H. Price, however, in *Perception* (London: Methuen, 1932) p. 255f., invites us to conceive a disembodied visual percipient and contends that such a conception is not self-contradictory.
13. Augustine, *De Enarrationes in Psalmos*, 88, 5.
14. 1 Corinthians 15.35.
15. Ibid.

CHAPTER 4: NEW TESTAMENT AND PATRISTIC WITNESS

1. See Dennis Nineham, *The Use and Abuse of the Bible* (London: Macmillan, 1976) which sets forth the general principles on which modern biblical scholars work. Although my perceptions would differ from his at some points, I would recommend this book as an admirably clear statement of what needs to be said on the subject in the Church today.
2. Isaiah 40.8.
3. John 9.2.
4. John 9.3.
5. John 9.6f.
6. Malachi 4.5 (NEB).
7. Matthew 17.9 — 13; f. 11.14 — 15.
8. Matthew 16.13 — 15; f. Mark 8.27f, Luke 9.18f.
9. Matthew 11.15.
10. John 1.21.
11. Luke 9.7f.
12. Tertullian, *De carnis resurrectione*, 1.
13. Tertullian, *De anima*, 28-35.
14. 2 Kings 2.11.
15. Thomas Aquinas, *Quaestiones disputatae, De potentia*, q.3, a.10.
16. Augustine *De Civitate Dei*, 22, 28.
17. Lactantius, *Divinae Institutiones*, 7, 23.
18. Nemesius, *De natura hominis*, 38.
19. Epiphanius, *Panarion*, 48, 10. The term *hyperanthrōpos* that Epiphanius uses here occurs also in Lucian, whence Nietzsche probably drew his celebrated word: *Uebermensch*.
20. Origen, *Contra Celsum*, 7. 32.
21. Gregory of Nyssa, *De anima et resurrectione*, in Migne, *P.G.* 46, 108D
22. Origen, *De principiis*, 2, 2, 2.
23. Plato, *Timaeus* 58D; cf. *Phaedo* 111A.

24. *De principiis*, 3,6,6.; cf. Aristotle, *De caelo* 270b.
25. Irenaeus, *Adversus omnes haereses*, 2, 33, 5; cf. 2, 34, 1. This work was directed especially against the Gnostics, more particularly those espousing the system of Valentinus.
26. Tertullian, *De carnis resurrectione*, 63.
27. Ibid, 60.
28. Matthew 22.30, Mark 12.25, Luke 20.35.
29. Tertullian, *De carnis resurrectione*, 62.
30. Tertullian, *De carnis resurrectione*, 60.
31. See, e.g., Gregory of Nyssa, loc.cit.
32. See, for example, J. Munck, *Untersuchen über Klemens von Alexandria* Stuttgart: 1933) pp.224 — 9.
33. Matthew 19.12.
34. On Origen's theory of aeons, see *De Oratione*,27, 14; cf. *Comm. in Matt.* 11. 3.
35. *Comm. in Matt.*, XIV, 10.20.
36. *De principiis*, 1, 4, 1. This passage, omitted by Rufinus, is cited by Jerome (see *Contra Johannem Hierosolymae.*, 16 and 19; *Ep. ad Avitum*, 3) and inserted in modern reconstructions of the text of Origen.
37. *De principiis*, 1, 8, 4. This passage is from the remains of the Greek text. In Rufinus's Latin translation what takes its place is a passage saying exactly the opposite of what Origen says in the Greek text.
38. Jerome, *Epistola ad Avitum*, 14.
39. *De principiis*, 4, 4, 8. Here and in the immediately preceding quotations I have used G. W. Butterworth's translation of Paul Koetschau's edition of the text (London: S P C K, 1936)
40. Jerome, *Epistola ad Pammachium et Ocean.*, 7.
41. G.L. Prestige, *God in Patristic Thought* (London: S P C K, 1952) p.279.

CHAPTER 5: HOW AND WHY REINCARNATIONISM FELL INTO DISFAVOUR

1. See, for example, Flavius Josephus, *The Jewish War*, 3, 8, 5, and Philo, *De gigantes*, 2 ff.
2. C.G.Jung, *Psychology and Alchemy* (New York: Pantheon, 1953) p.35.
3. I have discussed its role in Christian beginnings and Christian thought in my book, *Gnosis: A Renaissance in Christian Thought* (Wheaton, Illinois: Quest Books, 1979).
4. Among the Albigenses, two classes were recognized: (1) the *perfecti*, who received Baptism of the Holy Spirit by the imposition of hands and observed all the injunctions in their full rigour, including total sexual abstinence and a strictly vegetarian diet, and (2) believers, who adhered to Albigensian teachings in principle but were not ready to accept the precepts in their strictness.

CHAPTER 6: REINCARNATION AS AN INTERPRETATION OF PURGATORY

1. From the *Trattato*, as quoted by Baron von Hügel, *The Mystical Element of Religion* (London: Dent, 1927) vol.I, p.284.
2. Ibid, p.286.

3. Romans 8.28. On the prison motif in modern existentialism, see the long article by Professor Victor Brombert of Yale university, 'Esquisse de la prison heureuse', *Revue d'Histoire Littéraire de la France*, March-April 1971.
4. Clement of Alexandria, *Stromateis*, 7,6.
5. 1 Corinthians 3.11–15.
6. 2 Peter 3.12.
7. See for example, Robert Amadou, 'Louis-Claude de Saint-Martin, le théosophe méconnu', *L'Initiation*, nouvelle série, no.1, 1977. Dr Amadou is a priest of the Syrian Church.
8. *De Civitate Dei*, 21, 13; 21, 24.
9. Peter Lombard, *Sentences*, 2, 18, 8: 'catholica ecclesia animas docet in corporibus infundi et infundendo creari'.
10. Thomas Aquinas, *Summa Theologiae*, I, 118,2.
11. Rosmini, whose thought shows the influence of the Platonic tradition and also of Descartes, Kant and Hegel, was disliked by the Jesuits, some of whose teachings he opposed. His teachings were attacked during his lifetime and some papally censured. His five-colume posthumous work, *La Teosofia*, incurred the censure of Leo XIII.

CHAPTER 7: EVOLUTION AND THE CONCEPT OF REINCARNATION

1. J.McCosh, *The Religious Aspect of Evolution* (New York: Scribner, 1890) p.113.
2. *Solemnization of Holy Matrimony*.
3. *Edinburgh Evening News*, 15 May 1980, p.1 At the time of publication of the article, the Dog Aid Society was preparing for combat with the Edinburgh District Council.
4. M.J.Savage, *The Religion of Evolution* (Boston: Lockwood, Brooks, 1876) p.51.
5. Ephesians 4.13.
6. I. Kant, *Der Streit der Fakutäten* in his *Complete Works* (Leipzig, 1912) vol.I, pp.637ff.
7. F. von Baader, *Vorlesung über eine künftige Theorie des Opfers* (Miinster, 1836) p.25.
8. Ibid, p.21.
9. For some discussion of Monboddo, see Arthur O. Lovejoy, *The Great Chain of Being* (Cambridge, Mass.: Harvard University Press, 1948) pp. 235 and 272. See also Emily Cloyd, *James Burnett: Lord Monboddo* (Oxford: Clarendon Press, 1972) pp.161-168.
10. I. Kant, *Allgemeine Naturgeschichte und Theorie des Himmels* in G. Hartenstein (ed.) *Sämmtliche Werke* (Leipzig: Leopold Voss, 1867) Part III, Conclusion, p.344.
11. Albert Schweitzer, *Reverence for Life*, T. Kiernan (ed.) (New York: Philosophical Library, 1965) p.72. This is an anthology of selected writtings.
12. Albert Schweitzer, *Indian Thought and Its Development* (Boston: Beacon Press, 1952) pp.222f.
13. Emory Ross in *The Saturday Review* 25 September 1965, (Schweitzer memorial issue).

CHAPTER 8: ANGELS AND OTHER MINISTERS OF THE GRACE OF GOD

1. Luke 1.26–38.
2. Revelation 12.7–9.
3. Matthew 26.53 (JB).
4. *Shepherd*, Mandate 6, 2, 1–3.
5. *Phaedo* 108 B.
6. Ambrose, *In Ps.* 37.43.
7. 1 Peter 5.8 (JB).
8. 1 Peter 5.9 (JB).
9. Philippians 2.12.
10. Psalm 91.11–12.
11. Deuteronomy 6.16 f. Matthew 4.7, Luke 4.12.
12. Matthew, 4.11, Mark 1.13.
13. Hebrew 12.1.
14. Origen, *On Prayer*, in J. E. L. Oulton and H. Chadwick, *Alexandrian Christianity* (Library of Christian Classics) (Philadelphia: Westminster Press, 1954) p.325.

CHAPTER 9: MEMORY AND CLAIMS OF RECOLLECTION OF PREVIOUS LIVES

1. Charles Richet, *Thirty Years of Psychical Research* (London: Macmillan, 1923) p.607. (English translation of his *Traité de Métapsychique*). See also a review by Sir Oliver Lodge in *Proceedings of the Society for Psychical Research*, vol.XXXIV, pp.70–106.
2. A conventional distinction in regard to the concept of memory is: (a) registration, (b) retention and (c) recall.
3. Influence from *Little Red Riding Hood* may be ruled out, not only because I remember making its acquaintance for the first time at a later date, but also because the wolf was perceived by me as unambiguously male.
4. John Henry Newman, *Apologia pro vita sua* (New York: The Modern Library, 1950) pp.34f.
5. Hebrews 13.14.

CHAPTER 10: REINCARNATION IN EUROPEAN AND AMERICAN LITERATURE SINCE THE RENAISSANCE

1. W. R. Inge, *The Platonic Tradition in English Religious Thought* (London: Longmans, Green, 1926) p.65.
2. Edmund Spenser, *The Faerie Queene*, Book III, Canto 6.
3. William Shakespeare, *Hamlet*, Act III, Scene 1.
4. John Donne, *The Progress of the Soul*, (New York: Modern Library, 1941) p.218.
5. John Milton, *On the Death of a Fair Infant Dying of a Cough*. In *The Poetical Works of John Milton* (London: Macmillan, 1880) p.480.
6. Jean Paul Richter, *Selina*. In *Werke* (Berlin and Stuttgart: Paul Nerrlich, n.d.) vol.I, p.lxvii.

7. *The Works of Edgar Allan Poe* (New York: Collier, 1903) vol.II, p.361.

8. In earlier editions of Masefield's poem, *A Creed*, quoted in the opening to this chapter, the opening phrase read: 'I held'. See *The Collected Poems of John Masefield* (London: William Heinemann, 1923) p.69. This seems to have been a departure from the original text; at any rate, from 1935 the words 'I hold' are used.

9. Conversation as reported in *Lord Riddell's Intimate Diary of the Peace Conference and After* (London: Victor Gollancz, 1953) pp.122f.

CHAPTER 11: PHILOSOPHICAL OBJECTIONS AND REFLECTIONS

1. For discussions of this question see the following papers: J. J. C. Smart, 'Sensations and Brain Processes', in V. C. Chappell (ed.) *The Philosophy of Mind*, (Englewood Cliffs, N.J: Prentice-Hall, 1962) pp.160–72 (a revision of an earlier form of the same paper that had appeared in *The Philosophical Review*, vol.LXVIII, 1959), and Jerome Shaffer, 'Could Mental States Be Brain Processes?', in *The Journal of Philosophy*, vol.LVIII, 26 (1961) pp.813–22. Also important and relevant to the subject of the present chapter are: Brand Blanshard, *The Nature of Thought* (London: George Allen and Unwin, 1939); vol.I. C. D. Broad, *The Mind and Its Place in Nature* (London: Routledge and Kegan Paul, 1925); Peter Laslett (ed.), *The Physical Basis of Mind* (Oxford: Blackwell, 1951); H. D. Lewis, 'Mind and Body', in *Clarity is Not Enough* (London: George Allen and Unwin, 1963); Gilbert Ryle, *The Concept of Mind* (London: Hutchinson, 1949); P. F. Strawson, *Individuals* (London: Methuen, 1959); John Wisdom, *Other Minds* (Oxford, B. H. Blackwell, 1949); Jerome Shaffer, 'Recent Work on the Mind-Body Problem' in *American Philosophical Quarterly*, vol.II (1965), pp.81–104.

   For more recent discussion the following works should be consulted: John O'Connor (ed.), *Modern Materialism: Readings on Mind-Body Identity* (New York: Harcourt, Brace and World, 1969); C. V. Borst (ed.) *The Mind-Brain Identity Theory* (New York: The Macmillan Company, 1969); David M. Rosenthal (ed.), *Materialism and the Mind-Body Problem* (New York: Prentice-Hall, 1971); Patrick H. Winston, *Artificial Intelligence* (Reading, Maryland: Addison-Wesley, 1977); R. Rorty, 'Functionalism, Machines, and Incorrigibility', *The Journal of Philosophy*, LXIX, 8, 1972, pp.203–20; Paul Churchland, *Scientific Realism and the Plasticity of Mind* (Cambridge: Cambridge University Press, 1980); Sidney Shoemaker, 'Functionalism and Qualia', in *Philosophical Studies* XXVII, 4, 1975, pp.291–315.

2. Teilhard recalls his childhood fascination with the discovery that he could lose part of his body (e.g. hair and nails) with no injury to himself.

CHAPTER 12: THEOLOGICAL OBJECTIONS AND REFLECTIONS

1. A. C. Ewing, 'The Philosophy fo McTaggart, With Special Reference to the Doctrine of Reincarnation', *Aryan Path*, February 1957.

2. Philippians 2.5–11.
3. *Summa Theologiae*, I, 2, 2 ad 1.
4. John Hick, *Evil and the God of Love* (London: Collins, 1968) pp.345 ff.
5. *The Oxford Book of English Mystical Verse*, (Oxford: Clarendon Press, 1917), pp.463f.
6. *Philosophical Issues in Religious Thought* (Boston: Houghton Mifflin, 1973) pp.147–205. Cf. pp.425–61.

CHAPTER 13: THE LIFE OF THE WORLD TO COME

1. Isaiah 40.30f.
2. Henry Drummond, *Natural Law in the Spiritual World* (New York: Pott, 1904) p.303. The original edition appeared in 1883.
3. Matthew 7.20.
4. Corinthians 2.6–9 (JB) Cf. Isaiah 64.3, also Isaiah 25.8 and Revelation 7.9–17.

Index